C0-BWI-059

Sojourn In Savannah

AN OFFICIAL GUIDEBOOK AND MAP OF HISTORIC SAVANNAH AND THE SURROUNDING COUNTRYSIDE

New! Includes A Child's Guide to Savannah

Completely revised and edited by Dr. Ulrike Patzl-Träub

Published in memory of Terry Victor, Franklin Traub and Betty Rauers, three dedicated, loving and inspired guides.

© Copyright 1995. The Franklin S. Traub Trust

Ninth Edition 1995

THE OLD HARBOR LIGHT

—Drawing By Christopher Murphy

Table of Contents

—Drawing by Ray Dilley

OGLETHORPE MONUMENT

Introductory Sentences

by Anita Raskin

Cities are like people. Some are brash young fellows, lusty and loud, with rawbones jutting and sleeves too short.

Some are callow shallow hussies, all giggles and flirt and furbelows.

Savannah is a Lady.

A Lady is gracious, a thoughtful gentlewoman who keeps her treasures polished for the pleasure of her guests. Enjoy her jewel-like parks and squares, her prize collection of heirloom oaks, her matchless muster of 18th and 19th century houses.

A Lady is a hostess who sets a tempting table, with many good dishes from the old receipt book her great great grandmother wrote by hand.

A Lady never shouts. Savannah speaks in a soft southern murmur. Listen closely — she has marvelous memories to share.

Paris and London are her sisters under the skin. They share those qualities, so rare in America, of historical richness, architectural excellence, and the witty worldliness that comes of being a Lady With a Past.

Savannah is America's Mona Lisa. Gaze your fill, look all you will. (For once it's quite polite to stare.) You may never fathom the secret of her smile, but like those who love and live with her, you will know the endless rich rewards of trying.

Savannah— Georgia's port city

Savannah, set apart by attitude, style, and hundreds of marshy miles, has always been unique. A major seaport from the start, she has never been truly isolated, instead both welcoming and enduring a remarkable assortment of the citizens of the world.

The famous English colonists were not the first settlers. Roots of early inhabitants can be traced back to 3500 BC when the Biblo inhabited this area. Much later, a few years before James Oglethorpe arrived, the Yamacraws under their Mico, Tomochichi, settled on the high bluff over the river. These native Americans lived from the land and marsh, as did their ancestors. Oyster roast festivals today often take place adjacent ancient piles of bleached shells remnant from earlier feasts.

Savannah's history as it is told and celebrated today started in the early 1700's. On April 21, 1732, King George II granted the charter for Georgia to a group of Trustees, with the idea to help the worthy poor, strengthen the colonies, and increase trade and navigation, or in other words, develop new sources for England's wealth. King George's decision was further influenced by religious groups hoping to create a religious haven for all — excluding Catholics.

At the same time, Georgia was expected to protect Carolina from Spanish Florida. This early military connection has continued unbroken for over 250 years.

In November, 1732, the smallish, 200-ton galley ship ANNE sailed abroad with 114 colonists and James Oglethorpe on board. On February 12, 1733, Oglethorpe and his pioneers arrived at Yamacraw - soon thereafter called Savannah - and were cordially and ceremoniously greeted by Tomochichi, his Yamacraws, and John and Mary Musgrove, Indian traders. The Musgroves greatly assisted Oglethorpe in his early relations with the Indians.

Pleading his personal friendship and that of his immediate tribe, Tomochichi cheerfully granted the colonists permission to settle undisturbed on the spot selected by Oglethorpe for the town Savannah. As a by-product of the firm friendship which developed between these two aristocrats of such diverse cultures, Savannah flourished unhindered by the terror and warfare which clouded the beginnings of so many of America's early colonies.

Oglethorpe laid out the town according to a plan which he designed earlier in England. Savannah thus became one of the first planned cities in the nation.

The plan became famous and made Savannah famous. It foresaw wards around central squares, trust lots on the east and west sides of the squares for public buildings and churches, and tithing lots for the colonists' private

Panoramic View of Savannah, 1837, by Firmin Cerveau

homes on the north and south sides of the squares. The first church built on such a trust lot on a square was Christ Episcopal (then Anglican) Church, celebrated since 1733 as "the Mother Church of Georgia."

Part of the Trustees' plan for making Georgia a garden colony, dedicated to the production of silk, wine and other items desired in the British Empire, was the Trustees' Garden, located on the northeast edge of town. It was one of the first agricultural experimental gardens in the country. The climate ruined these ambitious plans and the garden was eventually converted to a residential area, which itself was the object of Savannah's first large-scale restoration project many years later.

Who were the settlers who came to this roiling new town? There were Jews, the first of which fled the Spanish Inquisition from Portugal and landed in Savannah in July, 1733. The founding of Temple Mickve Israel (p. 59), the oldest Jewish congregation in the South, goes back to this group. Later, Jews from all different nations settled in Savannah.

Joining the Jews were Evangelical Lutherans from Salzburg, who arrived in Savannah in March, 1734, and settled a few miles up the Savannah River at a place they called Ebenezer (p. 113). Groups of Scots and German-speaking Moravians were also some of the first settlers, joining the colony in 1735 and 1736. Savannah's ethnic stock was enriched by, among others, Dutch, Welch, and Irish, too. The descendants of the latter organize America's greatest St. Patrick's Day parade every year.

Preachers of the Gospel in the first days were John and Charles Wesley, whose precepts of Methodism have fared much better than the preachers did in Savannah (p. 40). George Whitefield came together with James Habersham in 1737 to Savannah, where they started the nation's first orphanage, Bethesda, in 1740 (p. 101).

A few important and unique regulations dominated the early days of Savannah: no slavery (till 1750), no rum (till 1742), no lawyers (till 1755) and no Papists, thus creating a paradise on earth (or not?).

These good-intentioned internal rules were not to prevent a general decline. The population diminished and crime was prevalent. Because of the failure of silk culture and with the antislavery law overturned, labor-intensive rice became a major crop; soon one-third of the population was slaves. Trade with the Indians fell off. Oglethorpe left Savannah forever in 1743 and the Trustees gave back their charter to the King a year earlier than planned. It was now up to the Crown to cope with these problems and thus the Colony became a province headed by Royal Governors, with Savannah at its center.

During the revolutionary period Savannahians raised their own protests against the perceived outrages imposed by the Mother Country, especially the hated Stamp Act of 1765, which taxed every printed thing and every official paper. However, Georgia paused longer than any other colony before deciding to join the revolutionary movements and participate in the Philadelphia meetings. The colony also hesitated to establish any representation in England, doubting it would do any good, but finally Georgia decided to take Benjamin Franklin's offer to represent her in London among other colonies.

Tondee's Tavern, at the corner of Whitaker and Broughton Streets, was the preferred meeting place of the "Liberty Boys," a group holding up the common cause of freedom in Georgia. Much to the indignant outrage of Royal Governor Wright, a liberty pole was erected in front of the tavern in 1775. In 1776 those at the tavern celebrated with numerous readings the new Declaration of Independence, signed by three men from Georgia: Lyman Hall, George Walton, and Button Gwinnett.

After the Constitution was enacted in February, 1777, concern was given to defend Georgia against expected British attack. And so it came. Royal troops under Colonel Archibald Campbell attacked the strong American forces led by General Robert Howe of North Carolina. The revolutionaries guarding Savannah were defeated. Once again in history Georgia was a British Royal province.

In 1778, French forces under Count Henri d'Estaing joined to help the Americans in their fight for independence. Some of the bloodiest battles of the war followed. One of them was the Siege of Savannah on October 9, 1779.

Famous patriots and mercenaries from European nobility were involved in this grim battle. The Americans were led by General Benjamin Lincoln, who was joined by William Jasper (p. 53) and Count Casimir Pulaski (p. 58). It was, though, another defeat for the Americans; shortly thereafter the British were commanding the whole South. In October, 1781, however, the English sword of surrender was presented to Lincoln at Yorktown, Virginia, and Savannah's liberation was near.

Nathanael Greene (p. 44, 80), commander of the revolutionary troops in the South, sent "Mad" Anthony Wayne with some troops to retake Savannah in 1782. The British evacuated Savannah and the Loyalists scurried back to England. On July 11 the Georgia legion received the keys to the city. After the revolution Savannah was the capital city of Georgia until 1786, when Augusta, and later Atlanta, assumed Savannah's role.

One of the highlights in post-revolutionary times was the visit of President George Washington to Savannah in 1791. He was welcomed as a hero and celebrated by all with patriotic and festive ceremonies, including a parade, dinners, and even a ball. Later, he sent to the Chatham Artillery (p. 43) a thank-you gift of two cannon used at Yorktown (p. 42).

Nathanael Greene received for his service during the Revolution Mulberry Grove Plantation, up the Savannah River. After he died of a sunstroke in 1786 his widow Catherine "Caty" Greene ran the plantation. President Washington, who knew Mrs. Greene from former times, privately visited her twice during his stay in Savannah. It was also at that plantation in 1793 that Eli Whitney, a schoolteacher from up North, invented, with the support of Miss Caty, the cotton gin. This revolutionary machine separated cotton from its seeds and made the harvesting of cotton even more profitable. With the institution of slavery and the invention of the cotton gin, Savannah's cotton industry was poised to lead the world.

Cotton and slaves made Savannah a rich city with a high society that knew how to celebrate and party. Cotton had become King and would dominate Savannah's fate until the end of the century.

Savannah was rolling in money when architect William Jay came from England in 1818. Jay introduced the Regency style to Savannah, beginning with the Richardson-Owens-Thomas House (p. 84). He also designed the Scarborough House, in which President James Monroe attended a party in 1819 during his visit in Savannah (p. 29), and the Telfair Academy of Arts and Sciences (p. 48), among other buildings and houses which were, unfortunately, later destroyed.

1819 was a year in which Savannah made worldwide news as home port of the steamship S.S. Savannah, the first steam vessel to cross the Atlantic Ocean. She left Savannah on May 22, 1819, and arrived in Liverpool twenty nine days later. From there she went to Scotland, and over Stockholm to St. Petersburg. In 1821 the S.S. Savannah came into a gale on the shores of Long Island and that was the end of that.

As glorious as life was back then, Savannah was not shielded from catastrophes. Two devastating fires in 1796 and in 1820 left about half of the city in ashes, including homes, businesses and the city market. 1820 was also the year of the yellow fever epidemic in which over a tenth of Savannah's population died. From its early days Savannah had suffered yellow fever epidemics, and 1820 was not the last year of this disease, which recurred in stages until the end of the century. Savannah lived through all these and other disasters, like hurricanes, always bouncing back to glorious life afterwards.

In March, 1825, the Marquis de Lafayette, who had fought with Washington years earlier, visited friends in Savannah to dedicate a monument to Nathanael Greene (p. 44). From the balcony of the Richardson-Owens-Thomas House (p. 84) he watched the parade, one of the many festivities held in his honor.

In the 19th century slavery was definitely both in vogue and indispensable for the cotton production. Cotton trade was made even more lucrative

A view of Savannah as it stood the 29th of March, 1734, showing Oglethorpe's famous town plan. Wymberly Jones DeRenne Georgia Collection, University of Georgia Collections.

with the advent in the 1830's of The Central of Georgia Railroad (p. 27), linking inland plantations to the port. At the same time the Central Railroad Banking Company was established. A monument to the founder and first President of the Central of Georgia Railroad was erected in 1883, symbolically displacing Tomochichi's grave in Wright Square (p. 45).

Rich and prosperous, antebellum Savannah was praised by many visitors as the most beautiful and tranquil city with magnificent trees and wonderful charm. The Georgia Historical Society (p. 62) was founded in that era and Forsyth Park got its artistic, cast-iron fountain in 1858 (p. 61).

In the political world tension between North and South was increasing. The economic necessity of slavery and the "natural" domination of the white "superior race" was emphasized in political speeches around town. Events climaxed when Abraham Lincoln became the nation's President. It came as no surprise that Savannahians danced in the streets when neighboring South Carolina seceded from the Union.

Soon thereafter, early in 1861 and three months before Charleston fired on Ft. Sumter, the Confederates seized Fort Pulaski, the supposedly impregnable bastion built earlier by, of all people, the young Robert E. Lee. In April, 1862, Fort Pulaski was attacked and quickly conquered by Union troops. After the war many said that Confederate Colonel Charles Olmstead should not have surrendered but fought the Union troops under General Quincey A. Gilmore to the very end. But Colonel Olmstead, when he saw that the modern rifled cannons used by the Yankees could easily breach the fort and send all his men to a needless death, conceded: "I yield my sword, but I trust I have not disgraced it."

Savannah suffered a sea blockade during "The War," one so tight that trading was made impossible. Goods for every day life were hard to come by. It was particularly hard for the Savannah Ladies...but for the Rights of the South they would, and did, endure everything. They formed several knitting societies to help their men in the fight for the good cause. And they were hard on every Yankee - male and female - even sometimes forgetting their good manners. They were, however, very strong and without them the men would not have been able to continue the fight.

In 1864, General William T. Sherman began his march to the sea. After burning Atlanta and everything else on the way to the coast, Sherman took Fort McAllister. Savannah was evacuated and thus avoided destruction. On December 22, 1864, the most famous telegram sent from Savannah was delivered to President Lincoln (p. 56), by which Sherman offered Savannah to Lincoln as a Christmas present.

With the arrival of Sherman's troops the war was over for Savannah and the reconstruction period soon began. Food was rare and the Savannah Ladies had to stand in food ration lines or take care of themselves since many of their men did not survive the war.

This was the time of the hated, opportunistic carpetbaggers, displaced freed slaves and the beginning of the Ku Klux Klan. It was hard to get freed slaves back to work since they wanted to enjoy freedom for the first time in their lives. Finally needing work, many returned to the fields as share-croppers.

Many others stayed on in town, though, and Savannah found its population swollen with Negroes. These new citizens lived in deplorable conditions, since white people did not want to rent to Blacks or would ask horrid prices. Social lives developed separately, though in many regards they were similar.

Great initiatives for educating the Negroes arose, but coeducation was not possible. Teachers from the North, trying to realize a long-guarded dream, were not welcomed by Whites and often had to live in the Negro quarter of town.

The support of the freed slaves for the carpetbaggers further enraged traditional Whites. A corrupt state government and the exclusion of the Rebel Whites from the right to vote enhanced the racial prejudice. In this fertile soil was born the Ku Klux Klan, which is still somewhat active today, although not confined to the South.

After "The War" and the fading of Reconstruction, the economy improved and cotton was king again. The city built the Cotton Exchange (p. 42), and for a time the world price for cotton was set here. Despite setbacks of fires, yellow fever and hurricanes, the city grew.

Social life was again important and people passed time playing golf, meeting at the yacht club or other civic clubs, and going to the theater and concerts. The most elegant hotel of that time, the DeSoto, opened, streetcars were running through the city and a railroad was built to Tybee Beach. The Telfair Academy of Arts and Sciences (p. 48) opened as one of the South's first public museums. Between 1908 and 1911, teams of the United States were competing with European teams for the Vanderbilt Cup, the most desirable prize in early automobile grand prix racing (p. 100). Savannah was prosperous and enjoyed it.

Blacks and Whites maintained separate lives. In 1878, the first public school for Blacks was established. In 1891, the first public college for Blacks was opened (p. 97).

In the Spanish-American War of 1898, Savannah was a major port of embarkation. A bronze statue of a soldier, facing south at the end of Forsyth Park to repulse invasion (p. 61), recalls those days.

Savannah entered the new century optimistically. New industries were thriving, including the export of ships stores like rosin and lumber. After the first World War, King Cotton died, victim to the boll weevil that destroyed, by the 1920's, half of Georgia's cotton. Thus came the bitter end of a delightful period.

Savannah was rescued from the failure of cotton and the subsequent national depression by the New Deal, some large industries, notably paper, and World War II. Fort Stewart with Hunter Field (p. 104) was established and with it Savannah's importance for the army grew. The mighty Eighth Air Force was founded here. Still today the armed forces play an important part in Savannah's economy.

Savannah's fame as a preserved and beautiful city owes much to the pioneering efforts of many Savannah women, among them Alida Harper Fowlkes, who saved the Pink House, Mrs. Marmaduke Floyd, who rescued the Pirates' House, and Margaret Thomas, who left the Richardson-Owens-Thomas House to the Telfair Academy. The first attempt at large-scale restoration was undertaken in 1945 by Mary Hillyer, wife of the president of the Savannah Gas Company, who convinced her husband to restore the company's holdings at Trustees' Garden. The financial and aesthetic success of her venture outwitted the skeptics.

In 1955, Anna C. Hunter and seven other society ladies saved the Davenport House from the wrecking ball, and Historic Savannah Foundation and its unique and successful "revolving fund" were born (p. 90). Savannah, with its largest urban historic district in the country, has recognized that its beauty is a priceless and unique asset.

Savannah was also the birth place of many celebrities. Savannahians revere the memory of Juliette Gordon Low, who was born in 1860 (p. 50). After an unsuccessful marriage she dedicated her widowhood to the Girl Scouts, which she founded on March 12, 1912, and which she supported even with her own money (p. 69).

Then, who does not know one of the many songs of Johnny Mercer? The songwriter grew up in Savannah and maintained family ties here. His Oscar prize is displayed in the Savannah History Museum (p. 26) and Moon River still meanders through the marshes nearby.

Charles Coburn (p. 57), a famous character actor, and Ted Turner, owner of the Atlanta Braves and a cable TV station, are no strangers to Savannah.

The unusual writer Flannery O'Conner was born in Savannah and brought up in Milledgeville (p. 68). Of Pulitzer Prize winners were the poet and writer Conrad Aiken, born in Savannah in 1889, and the still active journalist Albert Scardino, who was recognized for bold investigative journalism.

Finally and most recently is Justice Clarence Thomas, who grew up in Pinpoint, a small marshside neighborhood, and was appointed to the Supreme Court of the United States in 1991. The first Supreme Court Justice from Savannah was James M. Wayne, active in the last century.

Any history is complete when it begins listing the living, and so it is here. Step out now into the living history, wander the streets and byways of Georgia's colonial capital, and enjoy your own sojourn in Savannah.

—Painting by Willem Verelst

"TOMO-CHI-CHI, MICO OF YAMACRAW AND TOONAHOWIE, HIS NEPHEW, SON OF THE MICO OF THE ETCHITAS"

Architectural Trends in Savannah

BY WALTER CHARLTON HARTRIDGE

The buildings

During the years that have passed since Oglethorpe marked off its first streets and squares in 1733, Savannah has developed into a city of architectural distinction. Fine examples of a number of styles, especially the Regency and the Greek revival, were designed by architects of national reputation, and beside them were placed buildings that reflect a vigorous local tradition. All are shown to advantage by Oglethorpe's imaginative town plan with its sequence of squares, straight avenues, and orderly arrangement of lots.

Savannah's first buildings were the work of carpenters and joiners who had come out with Oglethorpe. These houses were all alike, of wood, one story high, measuring sixteen by twenty-two feet (see map, on page 11)— suitable habitations for colonists beginning life in the New World on the terms of equality prescribed by the Charter of Georgia. This house plan, with few changes, was carried far into the next century.

But colonial officials did not entrust the design of public buildings to Savannahians. Plans for the church were sent from England by Henry Flitcroft, a member of the Board of Works, who had built several London parish churches. Those for the Orphan House of Bethesda were supplied by an English draftsman known to posterity only as Mr. Day. Bethesda's founder, the evangelist George Whitefield, successfully wrestled with the difficulties involved in executing his ambitious scheme in a primitive colony. Completed in 1742, the Orphan House remained throughout the colonial period Georgia's most imposing structure, a high-roofed building with a colonnaded piazza which Whitefield described as "wonderfully convenient in the Heat of Summer."

After the Revolution Savannah entered into a period of prosperity and rapid growth. On a plantation outside the town Eli Whitney invented a cotton gin that made practical the large-scale cultivation of cotton; and with cotton enthroned as king in the back country Savannah became a great port. Leadership passed from idealists like Oglethorpe and Whitefield to a vigorous group of merchants from England, Scotland, and the Northern states. These newcomers scorned the simple dwellings that had survived from colonial days, and called upon the local builders to house them in suitable style. The Savannah mechanics were handicapped by the lack of a sophisticated tradition but, working from books of design, they built several handsome houses that compared favorably with those of experienced architects in the older colonies. The only building that survives from this time is the residence of James Habersham, Jr., called the Pink House (p. 40).

In 1796 two-thirds of Savannah was destroyed by fire; and as news of the disaster spread, builders set out from the North and Europe to help rebuild the town. The influence of artisans from New York is evident throughout the older sections of Savannah, in stoops and dormer windows, while gambrel roofs (p. 37), characteristic of Rhode Island, and light porticoes derived from Bulfinch attest the activities of New England builders.

Now for the first time a man who styled himself architect took up residence in Savannah. In 1797 Adrian Boucher, one of that numerous body of refugees from the French Revolution whose cultivated tastes enriched so many aspects of American life, moved from New York, where he had work-ed for several years, and offered to "undertake all kinds of Building, as Water Machines, Houses, in Timber or Masonry, in the manner the most elegant and strong." During the next decade Boucher never lacked for work. He planned the Exchange, which succeeded Mr. Day's Orphan House as the largest building in Georgia, the second edifice of Christ Church, and several houses for merchants.

When Boucher left Savannah, as the result of an altercation with the city fathers over his right to receive free Negroes in the ballroom of his house, the Savannah master builders came once more into their own. Having band-ed together for professional and social purposes into the Savannah Mechanics Association, they took great strides under the leadership of John H. Ash, a Savannahian born and trained, and Isaiah Davenport, a New Englander who had come south after completing his apprenticeship as a builder. These two men built a number of brick houses in the late Georgian and Federal styles, with high basements necessitated by Savannah's sandy, unpaved streets.

But Savannahians were still reluctant to entrust the local workmen with important commissions. In 1816 the congregation of the Independent Presbyterian Church, the wealthiest in Georgia, with $120,000 to expend on a new meetinghouse, offered a premium to architects throughout the country for the best plan. They chose one submitted by John Holden Greene of Rhode Island. Greene, borrowing from Gibbs and Bulfinch and adding deft touches of his own, designed and built for them a church that ranked among the finest American buildings of its day. Completely destroyed by fire in 1889, the structure was replaced by a building that is a duplicate of the original one (p. 51).

In 1817 the cotton merchants, now in their heyday, brought a talented young English architect, William Jay, from London to Savannah and plied him with commissions. Among the half-dozen houses he built—referred to as "little palaces" by the exiled Prince of Naples, Achille Murat — were the Owens-Thomas (p. 85) and the oldest part of the Telfair (p. 48). These and a theater, a school, a bank, a pavilion erected in one of Savannah's squares in which to entertain President Monroe, and possibly a hotel showed Jay's ability to handle Regency forms in a highly individual manner. Under his hand Savannah was turned into the "Southern Paradise" that one enthusiastic resident described, with stuccoed houses "as yellow as my letter, with elegant columns and balustrades, with Drawing Rooms full of Golden Eagles holding up Damask coloured curtains."

In 1820 Savannah was again visited by fire. Jay tried to persuade the merchants to build fireproof stores and houses of his design, but a severe epidemic of yellow fever that year thinned their ranks and a nationwide depression threw many survivors into bankruptcy. Calling Savannah "a Niobe of cities," Jay left for Charleston in search of clients, and in 1824 he returned to England. Hard times lasted into the 1830's. Visitors commented on the melancholy appearance of the town, and Savannahians who had come to take luxury for granted lamented the fate that had closed their theater and converted their sumptuous homes into boardinghouses.

When at length Savannahians constructed a railroad to the cotton fields of central Georgia the lean years were over. Savannah carpenters came forward with plans, welcomed by property owners, for tall row houses suited to the narrow lots that were part of Oglethorpe's legacy. These they built of the large porous bricks known as "Savannah grays" that were fired in kilns beside the Savannah River.

An Irish-born architect, Charles B. Cluskey, profited from Savannah's changed fortunes. In several public buildings of his design in middle Georgia Cluskey had shown himself to be a forceful exponent of the Greek revival style. His reputation was sustained by the varied work he undertook between 1838 and 1847 in Savannah: arched stores built against the river's Yamacraw Bluff, single and paired houses fronting on the squares, a convent which, in his own words, embodied "the principles of Catholic ecclesiastical architecture." A town mansion (p. 86) for Aaron Champion, merchant banker, is also attributed to him. This house later passed by marriage into the McAlpin family, who had grown rich in the manufacture of cast iron and Savannah gray bricks.

With Cluskey's departure to Washington in 1847 to work on the Capitol, important commissions in Savannah were shared between two successors: John S. Norris, a New York architect who is remembered for his classical Custom House of 1848-1852, and for the imposing residences of Charles Green, 1853, and Hugh W. Mercer, 1860; and John B. Hogg, a South Carolinian who studied under Thomas Ustick Walter in Philadephia and worked in both Greek and Gothic revival styles. Trinity United Methodist Church is a notable example of his style (p. 49).

On the eve of the Civil War, money, taste, and the skills of architects and workmen of differing traditions had made Savannah a "showy little city," as an English visitor called it. Oglethorpe's plan had been followed as the town spread over the flat land that extended back from the river. There were now twenty-four squares, eighteen having been added to the original six. The upper end of the town was hemmed in by a stand of ancient pines, and the City Council had set aside ten acres of them as suggested by Savannah's renowned scholar of Near Eastern languages, William B. Hodgson. In 1851 the tract was laid out as a park for which John B. Hogg provided a design in 1854. The streets remained unpaved and clouds of dust forced builders to make basements even higher than those of Ash and Davenport; but the squares had become wooded parks. Trees and buildings were brought to harmonious terms by Oglethorpe's town plan. This caused Fredrika Bremer, Swedish writer and feminist, a visitor of the 1850's, to exclaim: "Savannah is the most charming of cities... 'the maiden in the greenwood.'"

The broad outlook that Savannahians had acquired in their days of opulence did not survive into Reconstruction. Oglethorpe's plan was ignored in later extensions, architects of national repute sought no clients in Savannah, and even production of the local gray bricks came to an end when the last riverside kiln was closed in the 1880's. But in spite of the loss of many fine buildings Savannah still retains its character.

Architectural ironwork

Ironwork is Savannah's common denominator. The same scrolled designs appear in the squares—around monuments and fountains—and on the buildings which face them. Identical cast-iron balconies reconcile differing architectural styles: they are suspended from Greek revival mansions, Gothic villas, and Romanesque commercial structures. Stair railings and window guards enliven flat surfaces of stucco or brick, and give a fanciful touch to the austere row houses. Iron storks served as newels, iron dolphins as waterspouts, and iron griffins as foot scrapers. An iron harbor light guides ships into port (see frontispiece); and an iron spire tops the Independent Presbyterian Church, Savannah's most notable building.

—Painting by Leonora Quarterman

10 WEST TAYLOR STREET

Ornamental ironwork was a latecomer to Savannah. There was no demand for railings and gates until the rebuilding of the town after the fire of 1796, when ships that came from England and the North for cargoes of rice and cotton brought in ballast ironwork for Savannah's new houses. In this way William Belcher obtained the delicate wrought-iron balcony that he placed before the Palladian window of his residence on Reynolds Square, and Isaiah Davenport a railing and scrolled central panel for the stoop of his house on another of Savannah's squares. Ornamental ironwork was an integral part of William Jay's designs. He had used it in London and Liverpool, and from Savannah he sent to England for the handsome cast-iron balcony of the Owens-Thomas house. After the fire of 1820 Jay urged Savannahians to rebuild with fireproof structures. Floor joists would be of iron, cast into two lengths, united and supported in the middle by arches. Roofs would have iron rafters, crossed by small iron rods, on which tiles would rest. Shutters and sash frames of iron would give protection against both burglars and fire. Jay announced that ironwork for these buildings could be supplied by Henry McAlpin, a Scotsman recently come to Savannah who had put up a foundry on his plantation, the Hermitage, a few miles above the city.

Jay left Savannah but McAlpin remained. Weathering some lean years, he rode to prosperity in the 1830's when the Central of Georgia Railroad was completed to Macon. From the Hermitage Foundry McAlpin supplied builders with a wide variety of items: "Elegant Railing to suit either inside or outside stairs, Balconies, or Platforms, and likewise for Tombs or Fences, Firebacks, etc."

McAlpin never enjoyed a monopoly of the Savannah market, for Northern foundries continued to send their products south. Through a local agent, Youle and Sabbaton of New York disposed of "Cast iron Doors and Frames for Stores and Dwelling Houses, also Window Frames and Shutters, *as handsome as wood,* and secure against fire." But McAlpin was able to undersell competitors, and his industrial enterprises brought him wealth and civic honors. On his death in 1851 the Hermitage Foundry was closed. Ironwork from the North was placed on the costly houses that were built in all quarters of the city in the prosperous decade before the Civil War.

John B. Wickersham of New York supplied an iron railing to enclose Forsyth Place, the ten-acre park that the City Council marked off in 1851 at the foot of Bull Street. A cast-iron fountain manufactured by Janes, Beebe & Company, also of New York, was made its focal point. The design for this fountain may have been taken from one exhibited at the Crystal Palace in 1851, and castings had been sold to other cities in the U.S. and South America, even to remote Cuzco, where a duplicate of Savannah's fountain still plays in the ancient plaza against a backdrop of massive baroque churches.

To meet some of the demand for ironwork locally, David and William Rose, brothers who had been trained as machinists in Lancashire, opened

—Photo courtesy of Historic Savannah Foundation, Inc.

423 and 425 BULL STREET

Ironwork forms an integral part of the design of these paired homes on Monterey Square, built in 1858 for the Reverend Charles W. Rogers, Presbyterian minister and rice planter. They are taller versions of houses still standing on the west side of Gramercy Park, New York, which date from a previous decade.

the Indian Street Foundry in Yamacraw, Savannah's western suburb that had once been an Indian village. By 1854 they were offering "Iron and Brass Castings of all descriptions...at Northern prices." Large quantities of their work went to Savannah's three new cemeteries—Laurel Grove, Bonaventure, and St. Vincent de Paul—and can be identified by the firm name which the Rose brothers cast on their gates. During the Civil War the Indian Street Foundry was placed at the disposal of the Confederate government. The ironclad *Atlanta* was built there, and shot and shell were manufactured.

After the war, other Savannah foundries were established, notably that of McDonough & Ballentyne. But fashions change. As the century drew to a close the popularity of ornamental ironwork waned. A new enthusiasm for open spaces brought about the removal of fences from churches and squares; not even Wickersham's railing around Forsyth Place was spared. Now the pendulum has swung back, and Savannahians of the present day cherish the ironwork that has survived.

Well-known historian and author of the book Savannah, *the late Walter Charlton Hartridge served as an advisor to the city government as Chairman of Savannah-Chatham County Historic Sites and Monuments Commission. His article has been reprinted with the permission of* Antiques Magazine *and Historic Savannah Foundation, Incorporated.*

In Savannah... First

- Capital of 13th colony and later of Georgia, 1733
- City planned on an extensive system of squares in North America, 1734
- Agricultural experimental garden in North America, 1733
- Silk exportation in North America, 1735

- Moravian Church in North America, 1735
- Hymnal in Georgia, by John Wesley, 1736
- Lighthouse on South Atlantic coast, 1736
- Horserace in Georgia, 1740

- Cattle exportation in Georgia, 1755
- Newspaper in the colony, **Georgia Gazette**, 1763
- Negro Baptist congregation in U.S., 1788
- Public school in Georgia, 1788
- Practical cotton gin, Eli Whitney, 1793

- Steamship to cross an ocean, the **S.S. Savannah**, 1819
- Hospital for Negroes in U.S., Georgia Infirmary, 1832
- Commercially successful iron steamship, the **S.S. John Randolph**, 1834
- Use of rifled cannon in modern warfare, at Fort Pulaski, 1862

- Motorized fire department in U.S., 1911
- Girl Scout troop, founded by Juliette Gordon Low, 1912
- Nuclear-powered merchant ship, the **N.S. Savannah**, 1962
- Garden for the Blind in the Southeast, 1963

Walks and Excursions

Whether you are discovering Savannah for the first time or rediscovering your favorite haunts in Georgia's colonial capital, a tour of the "old city" is a treasured treat. Planned artfully from the beginning around now historic squares, the buildings and monuments capture in remarkable chronological sequence the flavor of a colonial, revolutionary, then antebellum past.

Amazingly enough twentieth-century life is wedded to these old city structures, many of which are proudly bearing the process of rejuvenation as their part in an ambitous city restoration effort. More enchanting than their substance — of architectural excellence, soft, old brick, remarkably wrought ironwork—is their significance, in quality and quantity, as a testimony to early America.

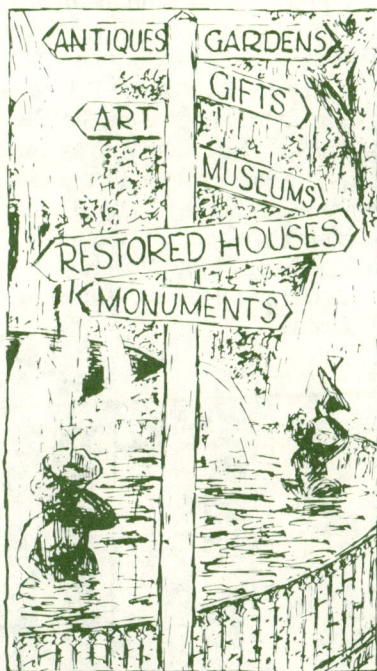

Go window shopping in the market place of history—but don't just walk and wonder! Be guided by the detailed directions which accompany the driving and walking tours on the following pages.

Those who wish professionally conducted tours may collect information by visiting or calling Savannah Visitors Center 944-0456 or by consulting Sightseeing Tours in the yellow pages. Educational and entertaining tours are available: mini-bus, convention bus, carriage; walking tours; harbor tours. Also do-it-yourself tape tours. Bikes available.

Stop Here First!

Let the Savannah Visitors Center be the first to welcome you to Georgia's Colonial Capital. Gracious greeters will provide information about Savannah: attractions, historical sites, lodging, restaurants, night life, sports, family activities and tours. Brochures and tour maps are available and a slide film demonstration gives an introduction to Savannah.

In the splendidly restored Savannah Visitors Center, lofty ceilings, handsome woodwork and graceful arches are creatively preserved with a startling harmony of Old Savannah colors. Rest here and then explore The Savannah History Museum. Its two theaters and exhibit hall dramatically portray the Revolutionary Battle fought on this site in 1779. Some examples of items on exhibition are the Central of Georgia's Baldwin #103 locomotive; a genuine cotton gin; uniforms, flags and weapons of the Revolutionary War, War of 1812 and Civil War, and an Oscar won by Johnny Mercer. In the two theaters two different shows are performed several times a day. Open daily 8:30 a.m.-5 p.m. Closed Christmas, Thanksgiving, New Year's. Special group programs. Telephone 238-1779.

Hours of the Visitors Center: Monday-Friday, 8:30 a.m.-5:00 p.m.; Saturday and Sunday, 9:00 a.m.-5:00 p.m. Ample free parking. Call 944-0456.

—Drawing by Leon Jay Meyer

**SAVANNAH VISITORS CENTER AND
SAVANNAH HISTORY MUSEUM
301 MARTIN LUTHER KING, JR. BLVD.**

How Not To Get Lost!

By making a quick study of the coded touring map in the back of the book, you can easily locate the intriguing historical sites described in the following pictorial summary of Old Savannah. Then you can visit these sites at your leisure—either by car or in easy stages on foot.

Later in the book, beginning on page 94, an area map provides directions for excursions to outlying points of interest in Savannah and nearby towns.

Walking and Driving Tours

OLD SAVANNAH: 1733 - 1900

(Driving Time: About 2 hours)

Visitors may complete these tours in chronological order by driving through the old city, guided by the solid red line on the touring map, or by following Walks A, B, C and D, which are also coded by color on the map. Landmarks #1 through #38 on the map are keyed to the descriptive material which follows.

Drivers begin their tour at Landmark #1. Walkers begin Walk A on page 31 at Landmark #4.

1. **SAVANNAH VISITORS CENTER AND SAVANNAH HISTORY MUSEUM:** As early as 1833 Savannahians proposed the construction of a rail line to the interior of Georgia. With support of the City of Savannah the first rails were laid in 1835 and reached, as their first destination, Macon in October, 1843. The passenger terminal, which houses the History Museum and the Visitors Center, was completed and serving the line in 1861. As part of one of the finest railroad structures in the country, it is an example of a Classical Revival structure with a long train shed. Savannah gray bricks, which were obtained from the Brikiat Hermitage, were used for the terminal and shed. The last train out of this terminal ran on April 30, 1971. The Central of Georgia Railways structure includes several remarkable, partly ornate buildings in red and Savannah gray brick to the north and south of this building.

BATTLEFIELD PARK: To the south of the passenger terminal lies the site of the Siege of Savannah, fought in October, 1779.

CENTRAL OF GEORGIA RAILWAY ROUNDHOUSE COMPLEX: One block to the south of the Visitors Center across Louisville Road at 601 West

Painting by Leonora Quarterman

THE SCARBROUGH HOUSE

Harris Street is the Roundhouse and Shops Complex of the old Central of Georgia Railroad. The complex, a National Historic Landmark, is considered to be the most significant, complete ante-bellum railroad structure to survive in the United States. It was not built piecemeal, but formed as a symmetrical whole to facilitate the operations of the company from locomotive repair and building, to transporting freight and passengers. Most of the buildings are from the 1850's. Noteworthy also is the exceptional architecture of the utilitarian brick buildings, designed in Gothic Revival, Classical Revival and Italianate styles.

It is an historic site with various displays. The museum of Early Years of the Central of Georgia Railways features antique machinery from 1833 on, including America's oldest portable wheeled steam engine; three model railroad sets and large locomotives are also on display. Picnic area. Self-guided tours daily, Mon.-Sat. 10 a.m.-4 p.m., Sun. 12 Noon-4 p.m.; guided tours 1 p.m. daily.

For more information call 238-1779.

2. **THE SCARBROUGH HOUSE**: North from the Visitors Center at 41 Martin Luther King, Jr. Blvd. William Jay, a 22-year-old English-born architect, designed the Scarbrough House for merchant prince William Scarbrough, one of the principal investors in the **S.S. Savannah**—the first steamship to cross the Atlantic. Completed in 1819, the mansion soon became a major focus of social life and was the focal point of colorful festivities during President James Monroe's visit that year. From 1878-1972 the house operated as a public school exclusively for children of African descent. Recognized for its extraordinary architectural and historical significance, the Scarbrough House was designated a National Historic Landmark in 1974. The facade emphasizes a monumental Doric portico projecting from an unadorned facade. Interesting is the location of the fan light which is placed over the portico. The grand atrium is two stories high, lit from above by a wide fanlight and skylight and supported by Doric columns. Behind the central hall is the ballroom with porches. Restored by Historic Savannah Foundation, Inc., as its bicentennial project, the building is now owned by the Telfair Academy of Arts and Sciences and, at present, is not open to the public.

3. **FIRST AFRICAN BAPTIST CHURCH**: West side of Franklin Square at 23 Montgomery Street. The First African Baptist Church and the First Bryan Baptist Church, at 575 West Bryan Street, come from the oldest Negro congregation in the United States. George Leile, a slave, began making missionary visits to plantations up and down the Savannah River as early as 1774. As a result of his efforts and the work of Rev. Andrew Bryan and Rev. Abraham Marshall, a permanent congregation was formed at Brampton Plantation on January 20, 1788. It was the first black missionary Baptist Church in Savannah and possibly in the United States. With the help of the Independent Presbyterian Church, the first Negro Sunday School in the U.S. was begun by the First African Baptist Church in 1826, and its present building was completed in 1861. The first African Baptist Church is the first brick building erected by Blacks in Georgia. The church has an outstanding sanctuary. The organ is placed in the horseshoe-shaped balcony at the back of the auditorium. Although no longer used, it is unique in design. Beautiful stained glass windows show the first ministers and leaders. The bell tower was once a lot higher but was knocked down in a storm and never rebuilt. Plans for the present building of the First Bryan Baptist Church were drafted in 1873, for a church on a lot which was purchased by Rev. Andrew Bryan in 1793 and which signifies probably the oldest parcel of real estate owned by Blacks in the United States. Although First Bryan Baptist Church

is not on the tour due to routing difficulties, to see it visitors may detour west down Bryan Street to #575 and circle left to rejoin the tour.

Franklin Square was named for Benjamin Franklin, once an agent for the colony of Georgia. Alternately known as "water tank" or "reservoir" square for the old city tank that stood there, Franklin Square was destroyed in 1935 when Montgomery Street became a federal route. The resurrected square commemorates the 250th anniversary of the founding of Georgia and stands as a monument to cooperation between the City, Historic Savannah Foundation, the First African Baptist Church and private benefactors.

CITY MARKET: To the east is the recently restored old market place. The history of this market place goes back to 1755 when the first public market activities were taking place at Ellis Square. City Market was one of the social hubs of the city which regained life again even after several fires and hurricanes. On today's location of the parking garage was a grand market building from 1872, designed by Schwaab and Muller as the architectural focal point of this area. Its tragic demolition in 1954, still mourned today, set the stage for later preservation efforts. The still-remaining warehouses and feed and seed stores, in former times part of the city market, have been saved and restored to give room to artists' studios, art galleries, a museum, restaurants, and clubs.

Drivers continue to Landmark #5; or, if they wish to explore the shops at Landmarks #4 and #5, they may park on River Street. Walkers begin Walk A at Landmarks #4 and #5 where ramps connect the two street levels and signs indicate shop locations.

FIRST AFRICAN BAPTIST CHURCH

WALK A

"RIVER STREET, THE STRAND AND NEARBY RESTORATIONS"

(Walking Time: 1 - 2 hours)

4. FACTORS' ROW AND FACTORS' WALKS: Strung along the bluff is Factors' Row, a unique range of red brick buildings named for the cotton factors, or brokers, who brought fame to nineteenth century Savannah with their flair for cotton commerce and their dedication to the Southern way of life. Still a focal point for much of Savannah's business life, these buildings rise two or three stories above the bluff and descend for three or more stories to the river front where, in the 1800's, the lower floors served as cotton and naval stores warehouses with entrances at several levels.

Ramps leading from the Bay Street level down the bluff to River Street are paved with cobblestones brought as ballast in early sailing ships; the bluff had no retaining walls until the early 1850's when city engineers began shoring the walls with brick and ballast to prevent erosion of the clean, white sand which surfaced the entire bluff and riverfront.

Halfway down the ramp, at the middle level, Factors' Walk stretches east, highlighted by the connecting bridges which lead to upper level offices and charming apartments that may be viewed later from Bay Street.

Factors' Walk and River Street below (Landmark #5) are popular for their diverse collection of specialty shops, galleries, restaurants and night spots—all housed in restored or reconstructed factors' buildings. Visitors who stroll down both levels will find surprises for everyone.

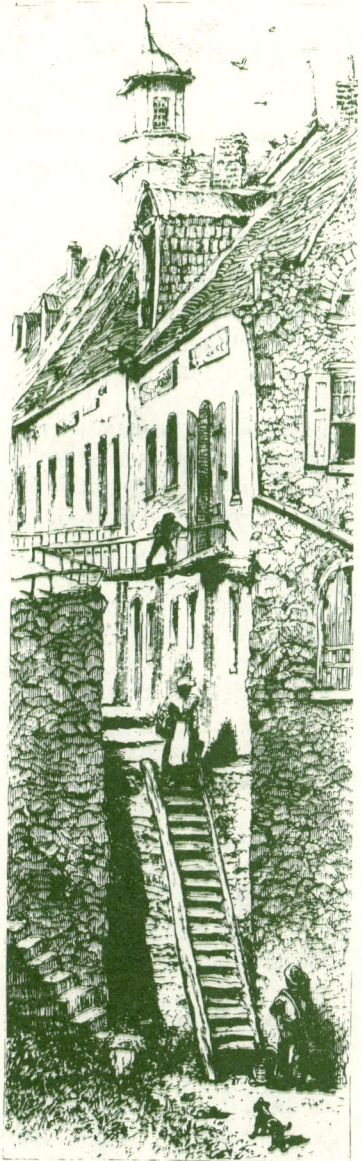

—Courtesy, Savannah Public Library, Gamble Collection

"ON THE WESTERN STRAND, 1870"

(31)

5. **RIVER STREET:** Cut through the wharf area during the middle 1800's, River Street embraces the incessant activities of a modern international port, retaining, at the same time, the aura of its former life. River Street's overhanging iron railed balconies and soft, old brick are enhanced by the John P. Rousakis Plaza and an array of shops, restaurants and galleries.

Train Museum: 315 West River St. Features "O" gauge trains on display from 1930 to current models. There is also an operating layout with a miniature village. Hours: Mon.-Sat.: 11 a.m.-5:30 p.m., Sun. 1 p.m.-6 p.m.; Telephone 233-6175.

Ships of the Sea Maritime Museum: 503 East River St. Models and artifacts representing man's 2000 year quest to conquer the sea; superior collection of ship models; Ship-in-a-Bottle collection. Open every day: 10 a.m.-5 p.m., closed major holidays.

Statue to Florence Martus, the Waving Girl: Florence Martus, whose husband left for sea shortly after their marriage and never returned, became an international personality. Between 1887 and 1931 she greeted the ships which passed the lighthouse on Cockspur Island, where her father was lighthouse keeper. She waved a white cloth by day and lantern by night, hoping to be the first to greet her returning husband; she died disappointed. To commemorate her friendly vigil, the Altrusa Club erected this statue by Felix de Weldon.

Rest here at Morrell Park before you climb to Emmet Park.

Directly across River Street is Savannah's Peace Pole, symbolizing hopes for "peace" in numerous languages.

6. **EMMET PARK:** Above the ramp, stretching for several blocks westward, Emmet Park is one of Savannah's loveliest vistas, a tribute to Robert Emmet (1778-1803), Irish patriot and orator. Within the park are points of interest which the more ambitious walkers may wish to explore by a small detour.

(Detour for those on foot; drivers may park.)

The Harbor Light: Placed 77 feet above the water in 1852 to guide ships into the harbor, the cast-iron beacon warned mariners of the graveyard of vessels scuttled by the British in 1779.

Eppinger House: Across the street, west corner of Bay and Price Streets. Despite its age, c. 1800, this valuable frame dwelling, with its long narrow porch running the entire width of the front, two huge chimneys and slanting roof with dormer windows, withstood its perilous transfer from another location. A nostalgia for the past mixes quietly with contemporary comfort in this lovely restoration which John Eppinger built almost entirely of heart-of-pine timbers.

Memorial to the Chatham Artillery: Close by in Emmett Park, dedicated May, 1986, to honor the members of the Chatham Artillery since its founding in 1786.

Vietnam Veterans Memorial: Continuing in Emmett Park, close by is the marble monument erected in 1990 by the people of Savannah to honor the men and women who served in Vietnam.

Celtic Cross: Next in the parade of monuments is the Irish Cross, erected to honor Savannahians of Irish descent.

(End of detour. Cross Bay Street and proceed east to East Broad Street, then turn right, continue to the left through the Trustees' Garden gate.)

8. **TRUSTEES' GARDEN:** Established as the first economic garden in the U.S., Trustees' Garden, begun in 1733 by the trustees who founded the colony, nurtured an immense agricultural experiment with plants and herbs from all over the world—and produced as its most dramatic offspring the famed cotton and peach crops of Georgia. Sold to Governor John Reynolds and subdivided in the 1750's, the garden became Savannah's first subdivision, preserved and restored today as Trustees' Garden Village and Fort Wayne Residence, two old gems in a new setting, picturesque, authentic and unique in America.

7. **FORT WAYNE RESIDENCE:** It embraces the site of Fort Wayne, constructed during the Revolutionary War and later named for General Anthony Wayne. At the north driveway, glance outside to the right at the retaining wall placed by the City when Bay Street was extended.

The Pirates' House, 20 East Broad Street: Housing a fine restaurant in a mysterious maze of rooms, the Pirates' House is a perfectly preserved seamen's tavern supposedly built in 1794 when this riverside section was a flourishing haven for sailors from the seven seas. Reminiscent of the days of wooden ships and iron men, the Pirates' House, once a museum, invites browsers to explore its peg-beamed rooms, nautical displays, local art exhibits and curio collections.

The Herb House, 26 East Broad Street: Probably built about 1853, the Herb House received its name when bottled herbs, reminiscent of old Trustees' garden, were stored here when the Pirates' House was a museum. Note the blue shutters, believed in early days to ward off evil spirits. To view the interior, visitors may enter through the Pirates' House from the parking lot.

—Painting by Leonora Quarterman

THE PIRATES' HOUSE-OLD SEAMEN'S INN—1794

Trustees' Garden Village: Built in the early 19th century, the houses facing East Broad Street from Number 36 to 58 shelter behind their beautifully restored brick and ironwork charming little gardens containing many of the original plants and herbs of the old experimental garden. Cherished as Savannah's first large restoration project, Trustees' Garden Village set the tone for giant strides in preservation which have been taken since its own emergence in the 1950's.

Crossing East Broad Street, the walker turns west on St. Julian Street to approach Washington Square. Drivers on East Broad Street merely turn into St. Julian Street, across from the Herb House.

—Painting by Leonora Quarterman

THE HERB HOUSE — 1853

9.   ST. JULIAN STREET AND WASHINGTON SQUARE: Washington Square, named for President George Washington, was laid out in 1790, was soon studded with small houses of great architectural merit, was later subjected to decadent slum conditions, and was finally liberated by talented and dedicated restoration experts whose brilliant achievement served as a harbinger of the rejuvenation achieved in Old Savannah. The square, neatly landscaped, presents itself as a garden to the surrounding homes, and St. Julian Street adds an authentic touch of the past with its surface of oyster shells.

For a closer view of houses on the south side of the square, walkers and drivers may circle the square completely before continuing west on St. Julian Street.

20 Houston Street: East side of square. Built in 1852-53. Small but privileged, with its construction of coveted Savannah grey brick, this charming house, now stuccoed, still bears interesting old earthquake rods.

Mulberry Inn: Corner of Houston and Bryan Streets. Incorporating an old cotton warehouse of the 1860's, the inn recreates authentic Savannah lodging of the late 19th Century.

520-522 East Bryan Street: North side of square. These double town houses with notable wooden cornice details and cast iron balconies were built in 1899.

21 Houston Street: West side of square. Built in 1852 by the Mirault family, French refugees from Santo Domingo, this house features unusual dormer windows with peaked pediments.

23 Houston Street: Following careful measurements and drawings, this c. 1803 town house was rebuilt c. 1964 to its original lines, retaining its old mantels and flooring.

International Seamen's House, operated by the Savannah Port Society: Corner of St. Julian and Houston Streets. A 1965 structure styled to blend with its historic setting, this hall and chapel offer a restful sanctuary to Savannah's many visiting seamen. Incorporated 1843.

519 East Congress Street: South side of square. As a two-family, twin-dormer dwelling, this house was built in 1839.

31 Houston Street: South side of square. Grey painted Savannah greys offset Victorian handcarved balustrades. Built in 1875 for Lawrence Dunn, designed by Augustus Schwaab.

26-28-30 Houston Street: East side of square. Note Savannah grey brick sidewalk, a hallmark throughout Savannah, linking these Victorian row houses built in 1887.

Recircle square back to St. Julian Street and go west.

512-516 East St. Julian Street: Double high-stoop frame houses such as these were built in the 1840's.

510 East St. Julian Street: Major Charles Oddingsells, Skidaway Island planter and owner of Little Wassaw Island, chose a style similar to many of the houses in Colonial Williamsburg when he built this house, the earliest on the block, in 1797. The distinctive bricks in this house were all fired in a kiln near Trustees' Garden and are shown to advantage in the large brick chimney serving all floors.

—Photo by Andrew Pine

HAMPTON LILLIBRIDGE HOUSE

507 East St. Julian Street: Across the street. Originally built by Hampton Lillibridge c. 1796, this three-story clapboard house was carefully moved five blocks to its present location and restored in perfect detail. As the only 18th century gambrel roofed house in the state, it is unique to Georgia and enjoys the prestige of being Savannah's "haunted house!" Among its countless claims to fame are its Captain's Walk, fine woodwork and paneling, old pine floors, black-green marble fireplace fronts, and exquisite furnishings.

503 East St. Julian Street: Typical of the first houses clustered off Washington Square is this cozy cottage with its single dormer, built in the early 19th century.

501 East St. Julian Street: A late Victorian house with eye-catching dentil trim, this home was built in 1901.

504 East St. Julian Street: Across the street, on the corner of Price and St. Julian Streets. Probably constructed about 1850, this house can be classified as one of the early elaborate 19th century town houses.

426 East St. Julian Street: Across Price Street to your right. Moved from a nearby location and restored, just as it was—including the odd-sized windows in front—this beguiling house typifies the design of Savannah's earliest modest homes. The six over nine windows, featured in the **Early Architecture of Georgia**, wide floor boards and rear dormer window add to its historic appeal.

421-425 East St. Julian Street: Across the street, on the corner, a charming double town house built in 1892 features brick painted green and marble steps.

419 East St. Julian Street: Reconstructed in 1964 as a fine, true restoration of the original William Pope House, first quarter of the 19th century, this house was sectioned into six apartments during its slum period when it was stripped of everything original except the fine hall staircase and old, wide attic flooring.

420-422 East St. Julian Street: Across the street. Heralded as one of the city's most beautiful restorations, this high-stooped Savannah grey brick 19th century town house featured in its garden an unimaginable assortment of ancient plumbing and a tribe of wild cats before it was so provocatively restored in 1960.

22 Habersham Street: Facing Warren Square, with its walled garden and marvelous side view bordering St. Julian, this late 18th century house was built by one of the Spencer brothers and became one of the most important, more elaborate houses of its time. It was saved from demolition by Historic Savannah Foundation's Revolving Fund, and then lovingly restored by a very caring and skilled young couple.

24 Habersham Street: Also facing Warren Square, on the opposite corner of St. Julian Street, stands a stately town house of noble proportions which was built by John David Mongin, owner of a plantation on Dafuskie Island, in 1797. The aura of its splendid restoration is enhanced by the stories of its historic uses—as a rectory of Christ Episcopal Church, as host to Lafayette during his visit to Savannah in 1825, and as a hospital for yellow fever victims during the epidemic of 1876. The garden gate often stands ajar, inviting visitors to take a peek.

410 East Bryan Street: Just off Habersham Street on the northeast corner of the square stands a clapboard house which is considered "a little gem" of the mid- 19th century. Built in 1848.

404 East Bryan Street: As the sole survivor of a type of wooden residence that was once found in many sections of Savannah, this house was built about 1822 by James Eppinger and recently was dramatically moved to this location and beautifully restored. Among the famous persons who lived in this home was Judge Peter W. Meldrim who, as a young man during Civil War years, banded his friends together to form the Bartow Debating Society—which had its library in the basement.

Continue down Bryan to Abercorn Street.

—Drawing by Ray Dilley

A GARDEN CORNER

—Drawing by Cornelia Cunningham Huffer

THE PINK HOUSE

10. **REYNOLDS SQUARE**: The tour circles the square before it turns north to pass the facades of the factors' buildings on Bay Street. In the center of the square Marshall Daugherty's statue of John Wesley, founder of Methodism, was erected by the Methodists of Georgia in 1969.

The Pink House: 23 Abercorn St. Known for the beautiful shade of stucco which covers its old brick, this Georgian House was built for James Habersham, Jr., in 1789 on a lot which was originally a land grant from the British Crown. Of Colonial architecture, the house is a good example of its time and one of the few extant buildings which survived the fire of 1796. In 1812 it became a branch of the Bank of the U.S. and in 1865 served as headquarters for General York. The portico, with a beautiful Paladian window above it, is of particular interest. The fanlight over the front door is one of the oldest in Georgia. On the inside there is a beautiful simple Georgian stairway. An early restoration, it now houses a restaurant.

Oliver Sturgis House: 27 Abercorn Street. Opposite the Pink House, the Oliver Sturgis House remains as one of twin houses of mirror image built between 1812-1813; an octagonal room was added in the rear sometime before 1819. This architectural gem was saved by Historic Savannah Foundation's Revolving Fund and restored to adaptive use by the Morris Newspaper Corporation whose executive offices bask in an elegant business setting of delightfully proportioned rooms with unusually high ceilings and intricate plaster work. The front steps of the house are the original marble. The wrought iron hand rails match the original. In the 1890's earthquake tremors were felt in Savannah, and tie rods were put through many older buildings. Tie rod plates can be seen on the front and side walls.

Lucas Theatre (p. 115): At the corner of Abercorn and Congress Streets. The Lucas Theatre was designed by the nationally recognized architect C.K. Howell and built for Colonel Arthur Lucas, one of the leading theater entrepreneurs in the South, in 1921. The four story building of terra cotta, concrete and steel is, with its wonderful ornate appearance, a unique and irreplaceable asset to historic Savannah. The beautiful facade and elegant interior are designed in the Adamesque style. The large lobby, together with the stairway leading to the mezzanine, is laid in Italian marble. The ceiling has a magnificent dome 40 feet in diameter lighted by 620 tiny lights. The decor is Italianate in style and technique, featuring extensive ornamental decoration. At the time of its opening as a vaudeville and motion picture theater in 1921, it provided the last word in theatrical systems and patron comforts, creating an ambience of fantasy and wonder. It operated continuously from its opening until 1976, and is now undergoing a restoration funded by a public-private partnership.

Follow Abercorn Street to the north, where the tour enters the Strand, or Bay Street as it is called today.

11.   **SAVANNAH COTTON EXCHANGE:** Before you approach to your left the Cotton Exchange, today the home of Solomon's Lodge Number 1 of the Free Masons, note to your right, on the north side of Bay Street, the **Revolutionary Cannon** which for generations was planted, barrel down, to serve as a bumper warding off traffic at a Bull Street corner. Close by to the west, the original **City Exchange Bell**, which hangs in a replica of the cupola, stands as a memorial to the old City Exchange, built in 1799. Flanking it are two urns which were brought to Savannah in 1858 by General Henry R. Jackson, the U.S. Charge d'Affaires in Austria.

The Savannah Cotton Exchange was erected in 1886 by William G. Preston when King Cotton reigned over Savannah, the Atlantic's major cotton seaport. Using the principal of "air rights," this is one of the first buildings in the United States to be erected entirely over a public street. This best surviving example of the Romantic Revival period exposes a rich melange of materials and forms, with its facade of red brick and terra cotta, iron window lintels, copper finials and copings, and turned wood posts between the upper windows. Enclosing the griffon and his landscaped fountain is an elaborate ironwork railing which immortalizes famous statesmen and authors in beautifully detailed medallions.

**SAVANNAH
COTTON EXCHANGE**

West of the Cotton Exchange a marker signifies the birthplace of the University of Georgia whose charter to its Board of Trustees in 1785 was the first charter issued in the United States to a state university. On the site across the Street the Legislature of Georgia met in 1785.

Washington Guns: Right next to the University marker. Paramount in importance and splendour was the visit of President George Washington to Savannah in May, 1791. The President was rowed down the river by nine American captains dressed in light blue silk jackets, black satin breeches, white silk stockings and round hats with black ribbons. Sparked by a boat parade, military salutes, formal dinners and a ball given at the Filature, Washington's celebration is best remembered for the outdoor noontide dinner where 200 citizens toasted their president as the Chatham Artillery fired its salutes in response. As a dramatic "bread and butter" present to the Chatham Artillery, Washington sent the two bronze cannon which had been taken at Yorktown.

GEORGE WASHINGTON

12. **CUSTOM HOUSE:** 1852. One block to the west, across the street. Designed by John H. Norris, the imposing United States Custom House is notable for its six monolithic granite columns with very unusual capitals showing carved tobacco leaves. Inside this beautiful example of a Greek Revival building, the double circular stairway has no perpendicular support for the marble stairs except the wall to which they are attached, but each step interlocks with the next.

In the third floor court room the famous case of the yacht "Wanderer" was tried, involving the last violation of the law against the importation of slaves.

A tablet marks the site of a small frame house which Oglethorpe used for his headquarters, sharing the limelight with John Wesley who preached one of his first sermons on American soil in 1736 from the city's first public building which stood on the rear of the lot.

13. **CITY HALL:** Across the Street. Completed in 1905 the gilded domed City Hall is a two-levelled building having two lower stories which face the spot where, on May 22, 1819, sailed the **S.S. Savannah** — the first steamship to cross any ocean. Note the tablet commemorating this historic crossing and its companion plaque, dedicated to the ship **John Randolph,** the first successful ironclad vessel in American waters, (1834). Inside, a large bronze fountain occupies the central court, over which rises a 30 feet wide and 70 feet high rotunda and beautiful stained glass dome.

Drivers turn south on Bull Street where the driving tour continues. Before beginning Walk B, walkers view Oglethorpe's Bench.

Oglethorpe's Bench: West of the City Hall on Yamacraw Bluff, a marble bench marks the site of James Edward Oglethorpe's field tent. Just as he pondered here his plans for Georgia's first city in 1733, so you may relax as you plot your pilgrimage to the past.

END OF WALK A

WALK B

"THE BULL STREET SQUARES: THE JEWELS OF SAVANNAH"

(Walking Time: 1 - 2 hours)

On the map walkers are routed south on Bull Street, through each square, to Forsyth Park where the route returns north, if you want to retrace your steps. One of the most historic walks in America.

14. JOHNSON SQUARE: As the first of the jewels of Savannah—the five little green parks that adorn Bull Street—Johnson Square was the earliest of the 24 original squares. Laid out in 1733, it honors Oglethorpe's friend and helper, Governor Robert Johnson of South Carolina, and remains as a crossroad in history: here the colonists came to find out the time of day from the sun dial (replaced in 1933 by the Society of Colonial Wars in Georgia); here they met to draw water, gossip and post public notices; here they gathered to receive President Monroe in 1819 and again in 1825 to laud French General Marquis de Lafayette, who laid the corner-stone for the imposing monument which marks the last resting place of General Nathanael Greene, Revolutionary War hero; here a public reception was held for Daniel Webster and his wife in 1848, and in 1860, upon the announcement of South Carolina's secession from the Union, a large meeting was held in the square where the Secession flag was unfurled from the Greene monument. To this day, the square is used for politcal rallies and other public events.

Supporting the busy life of the square, public buildings sprang up to link the religious, domestic and social life of the community. Foremost among these was Christ Episcopal Church, "mother church" of the colony of Georgia.

38. CHRIST EPISCOPAL CHURCH: East side of Johnson Square. Drivers may view church at this point or at the end of the driving tour.

In the very beginning, Savannah was founded as a Church of England settlement, and the nucleus of religious life was Christ Episcopal Church— under the leadership of its liberal minister, Rev. Henry Herbert. Later followed other well known clergymen, such as John Wesley and George Whitefield—both of whom added significant pages to the history of the early colony. With its simple dignity of outline, Christ Church is a perfect example of an early Greek public building. The present building, designed by James H. Couper, was built in 1838, replacing several others which had been razed or burned. Gutted by fire in 1898, it was rebuilt within the original walls. The impressive columned entrance, a graceful interior balcony and a beautiful plaster ceiling are among its architectural superiorities. Open to the public.

—Drawing by Christopher Murphy

CHRIST EPISCOPAL CHURCH

Close by stood the general store which faced the house for strangers, public oven and grist mill—all links with a past no longer visible.

In recognition of Oglethorpe's skill as a military engineer, the American Society of Civil Engineers dedicated the bronze plaque in the square to his city plan, naming it a National Historic Civil Engineering Landmark. A mosaic map near the sundial artistically reproduces the early city in colorful tiles.

Both the Driving Tour and Walk B continue south on Bull Street across Broughton Street — Savannah's former and hopefully someday soon again main shopping area — to Wright Square.

15. WRIGHT SQUARE: Named for Sir James Wright, last of the Royal Governors of Georgia, Wright Square was laid out in 1733. In its southeast corner lies a massive granite boulder, from Georgia's celebrated Stone Mountain, which commemorates the burial in 1739 of Tomo-Chi-Chi, the Mico, or Chief, of the Yamacraw Indians. The imposing monument in the center of the square was erected in 1883 as a tribute to William Washington Gordon, founder and president of the Central of Georgia Railroad.

The tour circles the square.

(45)

United States Post Office: On the west side of the square. Completed in 1898, the U-shaped three-story building is made of Georgia marble. Its architecture reflects an interesting conglomeration of the Spanish, French, Italian Renaissance and Romanesque styles. It is one of the more imposing structures of the late nineteenth century in Savannah. There are elaborate carving and terra cotta ornaments of highest quality over many openings, including one face of "Uncle Sam." The cornice is both heavily carved and inset with medallions of varying colors of marble. Loggias at various levels and delicate ornamentation put this huge building in perspective to its environment.

Chatham County Courthouse: Across the square from the Post Office, 124 Bull Street. Wright Square is traditionally the Courthouse square. The first Courthouse building on this lot was erected as early as 1736. The newly restored present Courthouse was designed by the famous Boston architect William G. Preston and built in 1889. The three story building with clock tower, built of pale yellow brick and terra cotta decoration, is an interpretation of the Romanesque Style. The Richardsonian inspired arched entrance on the West Facade has a terra cotta botanical pattern panel over the door and the date "1889." Buff terra cotta motifs occur on three sides of the building.

Bishop's crook street lights are placed on the Bull Street side. These lights are like those originally used on the street. In a restoration effort, most of the lights on Bull Street will be replaced by these lights; the sidewalks will also appear again in their original form.

37. **LUTHERAN CHURCH OF THE ASCENSION**: Rising on the east side of the square, the Lutheran Church of the Ascension is one of Savannah's most celebrated landmarks. Drivers may view church at this point or towards the end of the tour. Organized in 1741 by the Salzburger, John Martin Bolzius, pastor of the Ebenezer colony, the congregation worshipped for several years in a dwelling used as a hospice for visiting Salzburgers. In 1771 the present lot was deeded to the church and the first frame church building was erected in 1772. After the church burned in 1797, a second frame building was constructed and used until 1843, when a more substantial brick building was erected. The present church, built between 1875-1879, was designed by George B. Clarke, who combined features of the Norman and Gothic styles. Climaxed by the exquisite Ascension Window, the main sanctuary is one of Savannah's most dramatic church interiors. Visitors will wish to note, in addition to the Ascension Window, which depicts the Ascension of the Lord, and after which the church was named:
*Thorvaldsen's statue of Christ in the lower narthex
*16 episodes of the history of the Church in miniature

—Painting by Leonora Quarterman

LUTHERAN CHURCH OF THE ASCENSION

(47)

Upstairs in the sanctuary:
*Rose window depicting Luther's coat of arms
*On the sides of the sanctuary stained glass windows presenting the life of Christ
*Marble altar which depicts Da Vinci's "Last Supper"
Open to the public.

NOTE TO WALKERS: You may detour 3 blocks west on State Street for optional side tour to Landmark #18, as shown by dotted lines on walking tour map.

18. **TELFAIR ACADEMY OF ARTS AND SCIENCES:** Across Telfair Square, 121 Barnard Street. Designed by William Jay and completed in 1819 for Alexander Telfair, son of Governor Edward Telfair, this Regency mansion was bequeathed in 1875 to the Georgia Historical Society to be used as a museum. In the 1880's it was remodelled and enlarged into the city's major

—Painting by Richard Low Evans

TELFAIR ACADEMY OF ARTS AND SCIENCES

art museum, the oldest public museum in the South. Its rooms, which Jay creatively designed in varying sizes and shapes, display a fine permanent collection of paintings, such as American, French and German Impressionists, exquisite furniture, Savannah-made silver, and the original mantelpieces, moldings, cornices and innovations for which Jay was so famous. On every "2nd Wednesday" of the month are lunchtime gallery talks and films at 12:30 p.m. For information call 232-1177. Open 10:00-5:00, Tues.-Sat.; 2:00-5:00, Sun.; closed Mon.

Trinity United Methodist Church: 127 Barnard Street. South of Telfair Academy. As the oldest Methodist church in Savannah, Trinity holds a unique place in the development of world Methodism. Dedicated in 1848, the sanctuary is a true example of Corinthian architecture, designed by John B. Hogg. With an interior design similar to that of Wesley Chapel in London, the church is constructed of Savannah gray brick with a stucco finish. Virgin longleaf Georgia pines were hand hewn for the framing, flooring and wainscoating. Wall plaques immortalize the pastors who died while serving Trinity.

End of detour. Walk east on York Street to Bull Street, where Walk B continues with Landmark #16, south on Bull Street at the corner of Oglethorpe Avenue.

—Painting by Leonora Quarterman

TRINITY UNITED METHODIST CHURCH

—Drawing by C. Williamson

JULIETTE GORDON LOW BIRTHPLACE

16. **JULIETTE GORDON LOW BIRTHPLACE:** As a reward for its architectural beauty, historical significance and exceptional furnishings, this Regency mansion was named Savannah's first National Historic Landmark in 1965. The indented arches around the window over the porch and around certain of the windows in the facade are one of many fine details. At the east is a lovely Victorian garden enclosed by an iron fence. Now owned and operated by the Girl Scouts of the U.S.A. as a living memorial to Juliette Gordon Low, their founder, and as the Girl Scout National Center, "the birthplace," as it is fondly called, attracts Girl Scouts and visitors from all over the world.

Attributed to William Jay, the house was built in 1818-1821 for James Moore Wayne, the Mayor of Savannah, and was sold in 1831 to William Washington Gordon. It remained in the hands of his descendants until its purchase and preservation by the Girl Scouts in the 1950's. Open every day except Wed., 10:00-4:00; open 12:30-4:30 on Sun. Gift shop.

Walkers continue down Bull Street via Landmark #17 to Landmark #19.

17. OGLETHORPE AVENUE: Laid out and named South Broad Street in 1801, this tree-lined avenue was later named for General James Oglethorpe, founder of the colony. Originally designed with wooded center plats, this section was used as the common and as a burial ground by Jewish colonists. The handsome marker to the west was erected by the Trustees of the Mordecai Sheftall cemetery for the 250th anniversary of Georgia in 1983. To the east stands a memorial dedicated to Scottish forbears by the St. Andrew's Society of Savannah.

Drawing by Christopher Murphy, Jr.

INDEPENDENT PRESBYTERIAN CHURCH

19. INDEPENDENT PRESBYTERIAN CHURCH: Southwest corner of Oglethorpe Avenue and Bull Street. For a congregation organized in 1755, John Holden Greene of Rhode Island designed the original Independent Presbyterian Church in 1817-1819 as a finely proportioned structure of Federal design and as such it is one of the most important Federal churches in the country. The original burned in 1889. The replica was designed by the famous William G. Preston. Today's building, a breathtaking sanctuary of simple elegance with elevated mahogany pulpit and softly filtered light, is thought to be one of Savannah's most notable buildings. The four Corinthian columns of the sanctuary topped with hand carved capitals support an oval domed ceiling. The trustees sent representatives over the South in search of trees in order to have a single trunk inside each column. In 1885 Woodrow Wilson married Ellen Axson, granddaughter of the pastor, in the parlor of the old manse. The lovely courtyard with its exquisite fountain contains Scudder flagstones hauled by oxen from New Jersey.

(51)

At 12 West Hull as you turn right on Chippewa Square is a handsome enclose for the church's parking lot. This wall was constructed from stones and columns of the original church.

20. **CHIPPEWA SQUARE:** Named to commemorate American valor in the Canadian Battle of Chippewa, War of 1812, Chippewa Square was laid out in 1813 and is presided over by Savannah's most distinguished statue, a magnificent bronze figure of James Edward Oglethorpe designed by Daniel Chester French, with a base designed by Henry Bacon.

—Painting by Leonora Quarterman

FIRST BAPTIST CHURCH

First Baptist Church: West side of square. Organized in 1800, the First Baptist Church was granted a perpetual charter in 1801 by Governor Josiah Tattnall, Jr., and moved into its newly completed sanctuary in 1833. Served by many distinguished ministers, one of whom founded Mercer University, this church was one of few along the Eastern Seaboard to offer regular services throughout the Civil War. Remodeled in early 20th century. Open to the public.

Philbrick—Eastman House: Southwest corner of Bull and McDonough Streets. Begun for Moses Eastman in 1844 and completed for John Stoddard in 1847, this fine example of Greek Revival architecture served as a residence for a succession of notable families. Added later, the spectacular iron fence with its medallion profiles of prominent men is a treasure from the grounds of a former mansion. Part of the same ironwork also surrounds the fountain in front of the Cotton Exchange building on Bay Street (p. 42). The third story was added in the 20th century.

Savannah Theater (p. 115): 222 Bull Street, across the square on the northeast corner of Macon and Bull Streets. Since it burned several times over the years, little remains of the original Savannah Theater, designed by William Jay in 1818. Parts of the rear wall still contain bricks and the foundation of the original theater.

Walk south on Bull Street.

DeSoto Hilton — Nationsbank Complex: Liberty and Bull Streets. After reigning for 75 years as dowager queen of southern hostelries, the old DeSoto Hotel was razed in 1966 to make way for the DeSoto Hilton—Nationsbank complex, a composite of contemporary and traditional styling.

21. **MADISON SQUARE:** Laid out in 1837 and named for President James Madison, the square features a monument to Sgt. William Jasper, hero of the Siege of Savannah in 1779. The granite marker defines the southern lines of British defense, and Georgia's first two highways are honored by the cannon south of the monument.

Circle the square.

Sorrel-Weed House: Northwest corner of square. Attributed to Charles B. Cluskey, this exceptional example of the Greek Revival style was completed in 1841 and has been preserved as one of Savannah's most imposing mansions. Important features of the exterior are the arches, a double half flight of stone stairs, and the Doric columns on the portico. Notable ironwork surrounds the formal front garden and ornates the portico and the balconies of the first story front windows. The elegant house was noted for its sumptuous and merry hospitality.

St. John's Church and Parish House: West side of square. Treasured for its melodious chimes, its exquisite stained glass windows depicting the life of Christ, the superb reredos of Christ the King, and the present Wicks organ dedicated in 1983, St. John's Church, of Gothic Revival style, was designed by Calvin Otis and built in 1852-53 after its organization in 1840 and charter in

1841. Close by its present Parish House, the former **Green-Meldrim home** which was completed in 1853 by architect-builder, John S. Norris, for Charles Green, a wealthy cotton merchant. General William Tecumseh Sherman established his headquarters here when he gave the city to Lincoln as a Christmas present after the surrender of Savannah in December, 1864. After subsequent ownership by Judge Peter Meldrim, former Mayor of Savannah and once president of the American Bar Association, the Meldrim family sold the mansion to the church in 1943, which restored it magnificently in its original

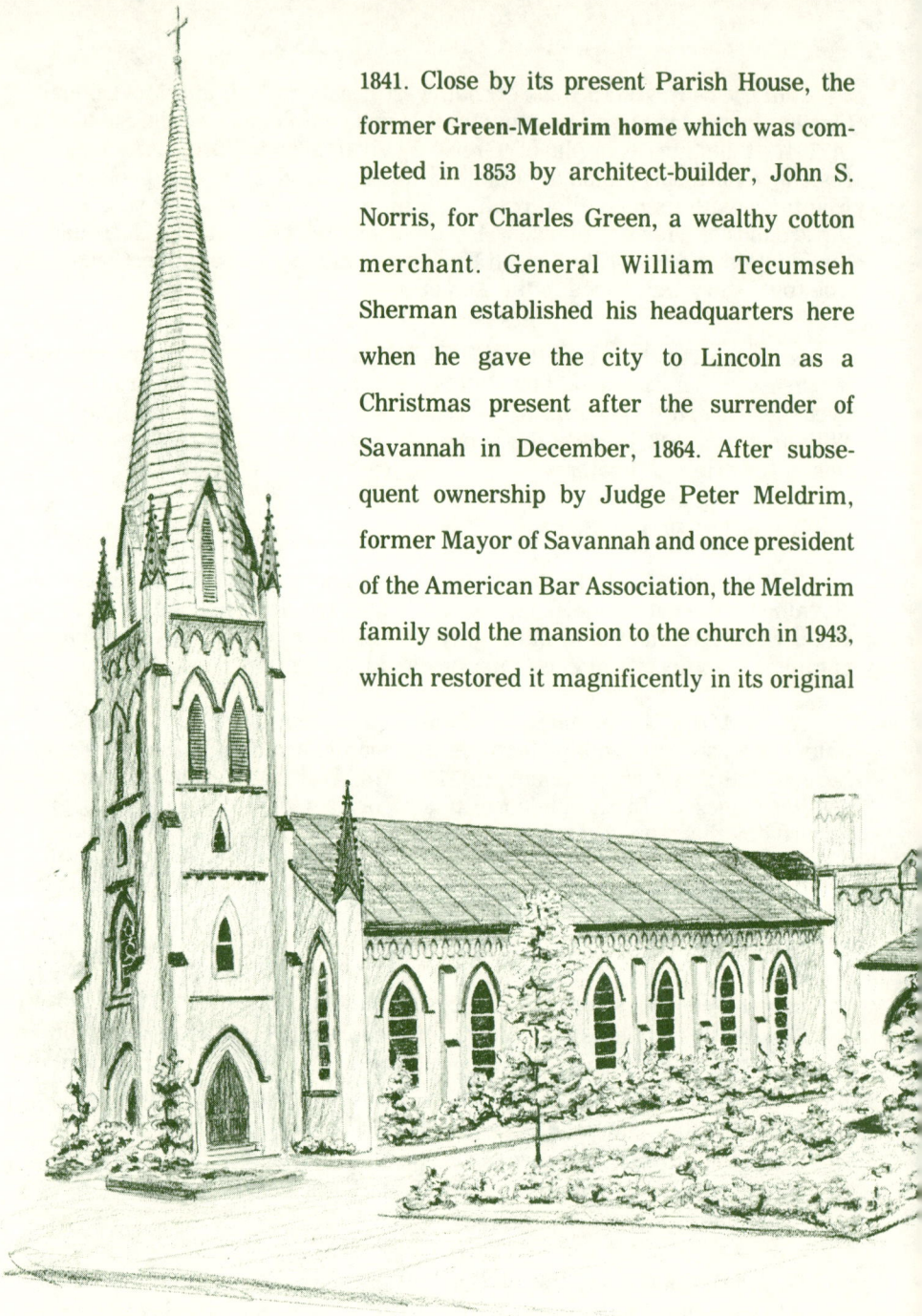

ST. JOHN'S CHURCH AND PARISH HOUSE:

Gothic Revival style. As such it is one of the finest examples of its period. The covered porch on three sides of the house is surrounded by ornate iron work. Note the oriel windows, which give light from three sides. The wood-work on the main floor is American black walnut and the elaborate crown moldings or cornices are stucco-duro. A curved stairway is crowned with a skylight rotunda, which could be lighted with tiny gas jets. Notable are marble mantels, together with other original adornments like the large mirrors in gold leaf frames brought from Austria. Open Tues., Thurs., Fri., and Sat. 10:00-4:00. Closed Dec. 15th through Jan. 15th, 2 weeks prior to easter.

—Drawing by Gerald Storey

THE GREEN-MELDRIM HOUSE

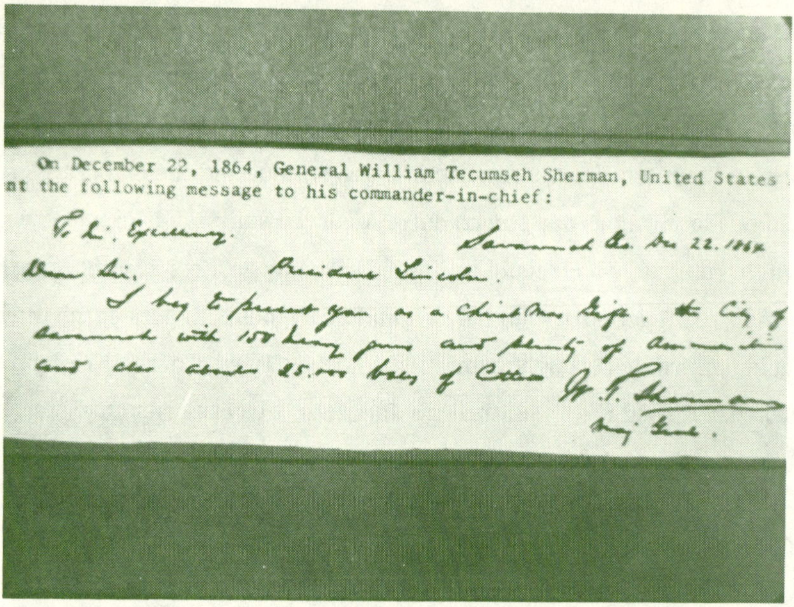

On December 22, 1864, General William Tecumseh Sherman, United States
at the following message to his commander-in-chief:

—Courtesy of Juliette Gordon Low Birthplace

TELEGRAM FROM GENERAL SHERMAN TO PRESIDENT LINCOLN: DECEMBER 22, 1864:

On December 22, 1864, General William Tecumseh Sherman, United States
Army, sent the following message to his commander-in-chief:

"To his Excellency   Savannah, Ga., Dec. 22, 1864

Dear Sir: President Lincoln

I beg to present you as a Christmas Gift, the City of Savannah with
150 heavy guns and plenty of ammunition and also about 25,000 bales of
cotton.

W.T. Sherman
Maj. Genl."

Masonic Temple: 341 Bull Street, on the southwest corner of the square
stands the old Scottish Rite Temple which houses a college bookstore and
restaurant. Note the Victorian decor and old drug displays, poignant rem-
nants of the very old Victorian pharmacy once sheltered here. It was a
favorite meeting spot for young swains who met to drink sarsaparilla.

Savannah Volunteer Guards Armory: 340-344 Bull Street. Across the street on the southeast corner of the square. The recently established Savannah College of Art and Design occupies the Guards Armory building which was designed by William G. Preston and built in 1893 for the Savannah Volunteer Guards, the oldest military unit in Georgia. The building, with its broad arches, intricate brickwork, towers and turrets is an outstanding example of Richardsonian Romanesque architecture. Decorative terra cotta and wrought ironwork ornate the red brick facade. The two cannon at the entrance were a gift to the Guard in the 19th century.

Offering undergraduate and graduate degrees this exciting college has become an asset to historic Savannah. Numerous buildings have been bought and restored for the college's use by the college and are yet another example of "recycling" of old buildings. A unique gallery at street level features the works of students and visiting artists.

326 Bull Street: Northeast corner of the square. The exterior is plain with emphasis placed on the triple windows on each floor. The house is the outstanding example in Savannah of fully developed Greek Revival style which reflects the romance of Savannah's most prosperous era when Charles Coburn visited often here on the square. Built in 1843, the mansion has been authentically restored and provides an ideal setting for an attractive shop.

Walkers and drivers continue west on Harris Street to Pulaski Square. Splendid restorations lead the way.

12 West Harris Street: The concrete porch with a cast iron balustrade was added shortly after the house was built in c. 1856. The rounded windows reflect the trend at that time for a more elaborate facade. With its recessed entrance it is one of the more elegant houses.

14-18 West Harris Street: Attributed to Charles B. Clusky, this elegant brick double house was built in the early 1840's. Beautiful features are the triple windows and simple Greek Revival trim. Note marble steps.

20-22 West Harris Street: Built in 1842-1843 this structure is a double house with quaint dormer windows. The houses have double high stoop entrances with wooden porches and porticos.

108-110 West Harris Street: Built in 1871 by Captain L.J. Guilmartin, this double house with high stoops and a beautiful cast iron railing was originally constructed as rental property, which was the fashion of the day.

126-128 West Harris Street: Remembered for Gen. Francis Bartow, who died at the head of his brigade at the Battle of First Manassas. This large wooden frame house with a wrought iron balustrade, a high stoop with sandstone steps, a three story porch and walled-in garden was built in 1839.

22. **PULASKI SQUARE:** Highlighted by Historic Savannah Foundation in its largest redevelopment project, the Pulaski Square area has become one of Savannah's most appealing neighborhoods. Laid out in 1837, the square was named for Gen. Casimir Pulaski, the gallant Pole who fell in the siege of Savannah. Drivers and walkers turn south, around the square. Note the new frame house on the northwest corner of Barnard and Harris Streets, constructed by a local philanthropist in the style of the period of the other houses on the square, in an effort to make the square architecturally "complete."

321 Barnard Street: Built in 1845, this wooden high stoop house features the dormer window-gable roof of an earlier period. The wooden fence reflects the simple lines of his Greek Revival plain house.

331 Barnard Street: Constructed in c. 1844 by Israel Dasher, this fine wooden house is a striking restoration.

215 West Charlton Street: To the west, just off the square. Built in 1846, the Moses A. Cohen house adapts itself to modern living, yet retains the craftsmanship and flavor of the past.

203 West Charlton Street: This simple Greek Revival house was built in the 1850's for Celia M. Solomons.

The tour continues east back to Bull Street. Note the delightful variety of mid-19th century facades on the south side of Charlton Street between numbers 25 and 9. Turn south on Bull Street.

1 West Jones Street: Facing Jones Street, with its splendidly linked row houses which will be seen later in the tour, rises the I.K. Tefft House, built in 1849. Internationally known as an autograph collector, Mr. Tefft extended his hospitality to renowned visitors such as Martha Washington's niece and the great Swedish feminist Fredrika Bremer who considered Savannah an assemblage of villas which have come together for company.

Continue south on Bull Street.

23. **MONTEREY SQUARE:** To memorialize the capture of Monterey, Mexico, in 1846 by General Zachary Taylor's American Forces, Monterey Square was laid out in 1847. Its monument salutes Gen. Casimir Pulaski, a young Polish nobleman who fell as a hero during the American Revolution. Circle the square.

4 West Taylor Street: Northwest corner of square. Built of Philadelphia red brick in 1852, this handsome home is guarded by iron cranes whose intriguing legend has entertained generations of Savannahians. The guardian crane, a symbol of vigilance, stands on one foot while in the other he clasps a stone which, should he start to slumber, would fall on the other foot to alert him.

10 West Taylor Street: Built in 1852, this stucco house is shown to advantage in an engraving of Savannah done in 1855. The handsome ironwork and Dutch tiled roof were added later, enhancing the exuberance of the exterior design and creating an interesting effect in contrast to the severely classic interior. See page 20.

423 and 425 Bull Street: West side of square. Built for Dr. Charles W. Rogers in 1858, this charming double house resembles one in Gramercy Park in New York City. Its graceful wrought iron, in contrast to the plain stucco walls, is considered one of Savannah's most beautiful examples of artistic ironwork. See page 22.

429 Bull Street: Cited as nationally significant for its architectural style in an Historic Savannah Foundation survey, the Mercer-Wilder home was begun about 1860 and completed in 1871. The house is outstanding for its cast iron window pediments, an overhanging roof with beautifully ornamented brackets, eight cast iron balconies and sidewalk fence. It was designed by John S. Norris and has been used frequently as a movie set.

3 West Gordon Street: Southwest corner of Bull and Gordon Streets. With dramatic artistry the heavy cast iron balcony and balustrade create a stunning adornment for this exceptional nineteenth century home where President Chester A. Arthur once visited his relatives. Initially a double house, it was completed in 1869. It is being beautifully restored at this moment by an antique dealer whose shop occupies the lower floors.

Scudder's Range: Southeast corner of Bull and Gordon Streets. Scudder's Range is a graceful queue of restored townhouses which were built in 1853 by the brothers John and Ephraim Scudder.

Temple Mickve Israel: East side of square. As Georgia's oldest Jewish congregation, Mickve Israel began with a group of mainly Spanish-Portugese Jews who landed in Savannah just five months after the founding of the colony. With them they brought a "Sephar Torah," still a prized possession of the congregation. Later, Jews of many different nationalities

—Drawing by Jemison Hoskins

TEMPLE MICKVE ISRAEL

joined this congregation. The present temple with its beautiful windows was
consecrated in 1878. Designed by Henry G. Harrison, it remains the only
purely Gothic Revival synagogue in the U.S. Early and recent documents
and art objects relating to Jewish life in Savannah and Georgia form a col-

lection which includes the original Torah and letters to the congregation from presidents Washington, Jefferson and Madison. Visit the collection around the corner on East Wayne Street Monday through Friday from 10:00 to 4:00 p.m. Free.

Walk south on Bull Street.

George Armstrong House: Northwest corner of Bull and Gaston Streets. Designed by Henrik Wallin and constructed about 1920 of a unique brick made from marble dust. The three story house with Italian, English, and French precedents was given to the city in 1935 for a college. In the 1960's the college was relocated and the building was sold for private restoration. It now houses a law firm.

Oglethorpe Club: Northeast corner of Bull and Gaston Streets. Built in 1857 in the Classical Revival manner for Edmund Molyneux, British Consul, this stately home was later owned by Henry R. Jackson and today houses the Oglethorpe Club.

24. **FORSYTH PARK:** Encompassing 20 acres, Forsyth Park was conceived by William B. Hodgson and named for Governor John Forsyth when it was laid out in 1851. Stretching southward from the Marine Corps marker, the main promenade is highlighted by the beautiful white fountain which was erected in 1858, and recently restored as a joint effort of the City and community residents. Following on the right is the Fragrant Garden for the Blind, a highly creative project of Savannah garden clubs. The lofty monument to the Confederacy, erected in 1874-75, was designed by Robert Reid of Montreal of Canadian sandstone and stands in Forsyth Park Extension—the parade ground of Savannah militia. Within the iron-railed enclosure surrounding the monument are busts of two Confederate heroes, General Lafayette McLaws and Brigadier General Francis S. Bartow. To the east squats a World War II dummy fort; to the south is the Spanish-American War Memorial. Outdoor plays and the very popular Savannah Symphony picnic programs flourish in this lovely setting.

Around the park numerous beautifully restored houses - most of them in various Victorian styles - attract for a small detour.

END OF WALK B

At this point walkers may follow driving tour to the starting point of WALK C or may return to the starting point of WALK B by turning north. Drivers continue their tour by turning west on Gaston Street. WALK C begins at Jones and Abercorn Streets.

25. GASTON STREET: With most of its stately old, beautifully restored homes, Gaston Street has regained its elegance of the mid-1800's.

20 West Gaston Street: Built in 1857 and once the pre-Civil War home of General Alexander Lawton, this stuccoed home features the romantic Romanesque touch, rounded top windows and brackets under the eaves—an unusual departure from the ordinary home of its time.

24 West Gaston Street: Northeast corner of Gaston and Whitaker Streets. This beautiful mansion was built in 1861-62 and remodelled as an Italian villa in 1907.

Georgia Historical Society: Southwest corner of Gaston and Whitaker Streets. Built in 1874-75 as a memorial to scholarly William Brown Hodgson, Hodgson Hall is the headquarters of the Georgia Historical Society, oldest such society in the Southeast. Designed by architect Detlef Lienau, it contains a priceless collection of historical documents and relics and is the source of most of the historical research done in Savannah. Open without charge Tuesday through Friday, 10:00 to 5:00; Saturday, 9:00 to 3:00.

The rest of the charming houses on Gaston Street were built in the 1850's and are unusual for their deep lots and front gardens.

Continue west on Gaston Street to Barnard Street, where the tour turns north.

445-455 Barnard Street: As the tour turns into Barnard Street the famous "Blues Range" houses may be seen to the west. Fine old row houses, they were built in 1852 by the Republican Blues, a still extant military organization that also acted as a building and loan association.

Gordon Block: Southeast corner of Gordon and Barnard Streets. Noted for its ironwork and unusual doorways—each house has a high stoop with fancy curved ironwork and interesting doorways—Gordon Row stretches a full block, 15 stately, 4-storied rowhouses built in 1853 for rental property and now restored.

Continue north on Barnard Street.

—Drawing by Ray Dilley

HOUSE ON JONES STREET

26. **JONES STREET:** Passing other old homes, the tour turns east on Jones Street. Jones Street offers a magnificent street vista of brick paving, huge live oaks and wide brick walks. Most of the beautifully restored houses in the entire area have historic markers dating them in the mid-1800's when paired houses, double curving steps and elaborate ironwork were fashionable. Crossing Bull Street the tour follows Jones Street to Abercorn, passing a stunning succession of high-stooped restored rowhouses.

Drivers continue to Landmark #27 by turning south on Abercorn Street. At this point Walk C begins.

WALK C

"ABERCORN STREET AND HABERSHAM STREET RESTORATION"

(Walking Time: 1½ hours)

On the map walkers are routed a few steps south, then north, then south again to their starting point. However, if walkers wish to follow Walks C and D consecutively, they may shorten their steps by observing both sides of Abercorn Street as they walk north, avoid the return to the starting point of Walk C, and join Walk D at Landmark #31.

As the tour approaches Landmark #27, it enters one of Savannah's most interesting residential neighborhoods, where countless examples of mid-19th century architecture are attracting suburbanites who wish to participate in the renewal of downtown living. No longer restricted to the very rich or the very poor, urban neighborhoods such as this one are expanding their perimeters street by street—gradually linking together the many pioneer areas where restoration first began.

128 East Taylor Street: Northwest corner of Taylor and Abercorn Streets. Built in 1860 of brick with a stucco finish, this house is one of builder George Ash's finest creations. Significant are its bay windows, marble porch and steps and brownstone window sills.

202 East Taylor Street: Across the street on the northeast corner of Taylor and Abercorn Streets. Enhanced by its striking ironwork, this beautiful dwelling was built in 1859. Of particular interest are its doorway, brick carriage house and garden.

Calhoun Square: Named for John C. Calhoun, eminent southern statesman, Calhoun Square was laid out in 1851. Detour hints suggest notable houses on streets radiating from the square.

426 Abercorn Street: East side of the square, on the southeast corner of Taylor and Abercorn Streets. Another excellent contribution by George Ash to the architecture of the 1800's, this handsome home is noted for its door-

(64)

way, high stoop, and exterior details. It was built in 1855. On the south side of the house note the wrought iron gate "camellia." Designed by Murray Galin and sculptured by John Smith in 1987-88, it features the beautiful and widespread Savannah flower.

421 Abercorn Street: On the west side of the square, a handsome house, owned by Wesley Monumental Church. Again, favored mid-19th century materials, stucco on brick, were chosen, offsetting a mansard roof, high stoop and marble steps. Built in 1859, it was remodeled in 1894 and c. 1920.

27. WESLEY MONUMENTAL METHODIST CHURCH: Corner of Abercorn and Gordon Streets. Considered one of the handsomest Methodist churches in the South, this Gothic Revival memorial to John Wesley and Charles Wesley, the founders of Methodism, celebrated its 100th anniversary in 1968. Patterned after Queen's Kirk in Amsterdam, the sanctuary was built in 1876-1890 and seats more than 1000 persons who may worship surrounded by the beauty of stained glass windows which were dedicated to Methodism's historic figures. The magnificent Wesley Window which is opposite the pulpit contains the busts of John and Charles Wesley who preached in early Savannah (at the Anglican Church) long before Methodism became a reality. Open to the public.

WESLEY MONUMENTAL METHODIST CHURCH

The Little House: 107 East Gordon Street. Across from the south side of the church. Coolly inviting, the garden of the Little House, a bookstore and gift shop, shelters the building which was built originally for use as a carriage house in 1856.

113 East Gordon Street: Walkers continue on Gordon Street east of the Little House to view a series of mid-19th century houses. The first—at #113—features a wood cornice and brackets, a balcony and cast iron balustrade, and a two-story porch. It was built in 1868.

115 East Gordon Street: Its doorway made important by side lights, pilasters and transom lights, this dignified house combines a cornice of wood with lintels and sills of stone. It was built in 1869.

127 East Gordon Street: Southwest corner of Gordon and Abercorn Streets. Constructed of brick and stucco, this 1856 house is distinctive for its high entrance stoop and bay window over the portico.

Massie Heritage Interpretation Center: 201-213 East Gordon Street. Southeast corner of Abercorn and Gordon Streets. Massie School, honored as Georgia's oldest school in continuous operation, is one of Savannah's finest structures—noted for its gable roof, wood cupola and cornice, and its unique connecting passageway. Designed by John S. Norris, it was completed in 1856; the wings were added in 1872 and 1886. This outstanding example of Greek Revival architecture houses a vital continuing education program, including "The Nineteenth Century Classroom," where young students experience a 19th-century school day, and collections on period costumes, state and local history, urban planning and historic preservation, and architectural exhibits showing the influence of Greek, Gothic and Roman architecture on Savannah's built environment. Open Mon.-Fri., 9:00-4:00 p.m. Phone 651-7380.

430-432 Abercorn Street: As the tour continues east on Gordon Street, a remarkable house built in 1868 faces the east side of the square. Among its many handsome features are the high stoop, curved stairs, portico and bay window, and lavish ironwork.

215-229 East Gordon Street: As the tour continues east on Gordon Street these notable late 19th century row houses appear to the right. Note wood cornices and brackets and brick segmental arch window heads, which were popular when they were built in 1872.

220-222 East Gordon Street: Just across the street on the north side of Gordon Street. Due to changes made during remodeling, these two structures appear to be different—while in reality they are parts of the same building. On the facade of #220 the balcony has been removed and a high stoop added, while #222 retains its balcony with cast iron balustrade and low stoop entrance, as designed in 1856.

224 East Gordon Street: An 1856 house with fine proportions, this home of the 1850's features brick flat arch window heads, overhead brick cornice and an entrance door with transom lights.

Beth Eden Baptist Church: The tour continues east on Gordon Street, passing the Beth Eden Baptist Church, built in 1893 by architect Henry Urban.

28. Whitefield Square: North of Gordon Street on Habersham Street. Named for George Whitefield, early Savannah minister and founder of Bethesda orphanage, the square was laid out in 1851. Surrounded by airy, playful gingerbread houses of the 19th century Queen Anne Style, the square is sparked by a gazebo for band concerts, which is in keeping with the Victorian "seaside" resort atmosphere of the neighborhood.

First Congregational Church: Facing the west side of the square. The church was organized in 1869. Its present brick Gothic style church, built in 1895, displays a fine gothic tracery window. The building has been completely restored, and recently the steeple, which blew down in a storm in 1940, has been replaced. The Congregational Church was very active in institutionalizing a Sunday School and kindergarten in Savannah for black children.

The tour turns north on Habersham Street to Jones Street.

400 East Jones Street: Northeast corner of Habersham and Jones Streets. A contemporary townhouse which echoes the materials and proportions of the surrounding historic architecture.

Continue west on Jones Street.

223 East Jones Street: Southwest corner. Cast iron grilles, lintels and sills adorn the lower windows of this 1866 house built by architect George H. Ash. The doorway, approached by marble steps, is highlighted by side and transom lights.

207-219 East Jones Street: Continuing west down the south side of Jones Street are other impressive groups of 19th century row houses.

212-218 East Jones Street: On the north side of Jones Street parade notable companions to the opposite row houses—many with converted carriage houses in the rear. They were built in 1853-1857.

204 East Jones Street: Built in 1859 for Abraham Minis and his bride, this elegant house is a perfect example of the English town house—of Savannah gray brick with Italian marble and doorways carved in the Egyptian manner. Stephen Decatur Button was the architect. Note the ironwork and a formal garden off the side of the house.

The tour turns north on Abercorn Street approaching Lafayette Square and turns east on Charlton Street. On Jones Street, continuing west, more row houses appear—further links in the remarkable chain of 19th century dwellings which line Jones Street. Walkers may wish to detour one block to #108-124.

201 East Charlton Street: Southeast corner of Abercorn and Charlton Streets. Notable for its ornamental cast iron balcony balustrades across the facade and its cast iron window grilles, this house of 1858 is an eyecatching asset to Lafayette Square.

207 East Charlton Street: South side of Charlton Street. The recently added ironwork enhances the high stoop of this flatroofed 19th century house, built in 1856, birthplace and childhood home of Flannery O'Connor, a famous Georgia writer. The parlor floor has been restored to its 1930's appearance and features now a museum of the author. Open for weekend visits, readings and teas.

Hamilton-Turner House: 330 Abercorn Street, northeast corner of Charlton and Abercorn Streets. This mansion influenced by the Second Empire style, was built by J.D. Hall in 1873 for Samuel Pugh Hamilton, jeweller and prominent citizen. This house is distinctive for its mansard roof, tall windows, vigorous mouldings and especially fine cast iron balconies. In the basement was originally a kitchen, wine cellar and cooling room. The carriage house at the rear is, like the entire house, built of Savannah gray brick covered with stucco. House museum. Tours.

211 East Charlton Street: With its gable and hip roof and cast iron window pediments, this stunning home is one of Savannah's most superior architectural treasures, built in 1853.

311 East Charlton Street: Built about 1873, this notable house displays a provocative balcony rail with simulated tassels in iron above clusters of grapes.

Passing notable houses with imaginative ironwork (peek around the corner to 345 Habersham Street to see the sunflower gate made by Ivan Bailey, a modern ironmonger), the tour approaches Troup Square.

28. TROUP SQUARE: Laid out in 1851, Troup Square was named for George Michael Troup, Governor of Georgia in 1823-27. An armillary sphere—an astronomical model with solid rings, all circles of a single sphere, used to display relationships among the principal celestial circles—is its central feature. Two marvelous rows of restored houses advance east from the square as part of a pilot Urban Renewal Project for historic preservation.

410-424 East Charlton Street: These eight stucco units, with their fanciful bay windows, were built in 1882 by John McDonough of the iron firm McDonough and Ballantyne.

410-424 East Macon Street: One street north, parallel to Charlton Street. The eastern four of these brick units were built in 1872 by John McDonough; the four units nearest the square were built in 1885 by Edward Kennedy. All are graced by particularly fine cast iron work.

Savannah Baptist Center: On the west side of the square. Originally located on Oglethorpe Square, this Gothic style church served the Unitarian Congregation. It later became St. Stephens Episcopal Church and was moved to Troup Square in 1860. James Pierpont, composer of "Jingle Bells," served as music director of the church in the 1850's.

Continue west on Harris Street to Lafayette Square.

28. Lafayette Square: Lafayette Square was laid out in 1837, soon after the Marquis de Lafayette, for whom it was named, visited Savannah in 1825. The city limits were extended to Jones Street, and the lovely houses which the tour stresses were begun almost at once.

At this point walkers may continue north, on Abercorn Street, while drivers circle the square to Landmark #29, unless walkers want to combine Walks C and D as mentioned earlier (p. 64), in which case this part of the walk should also be visited now.

29. THE ANDREW LOW HOUSE: 329 Abercorn Street. Northwest corner of Abercorn and Charlton Streets. On this site a picturesque old crenelated jail was built after the Revolution. Following its demolition, the property was purchased by Andrew Low, an English merchant, who built this elegant house in 1849. The home was later owned by Andrew Low's son, William Mackay Low, who married Juliette Magill Gordon in 1886. During her residence here as a widow, Mrs. Low founded the Girl Scouts of America on March 12, 1912, and in her will bequeathed the carriage house to the Savannah Girl Scouts. Graced with one of Savannah's most stunning ironwork balconies, this house, built of stuccoed brick, is owned and preserved by the National Society of the Colonial Dames of America in the State of Georgia—whose members and friends have donated its fine furnishings, splended old silver and the lovely three-tiered fountain in the center of Lafayette Square. Peek into the beautiful walled garden at the rear. Among the many "very important people" who visited here were William Makepeace Thackery and Robert E. Lee. Open weekdays 10:30 a.m.-4 p.m., Sun. 12 p.m.-4 p.m. Closed Thurs., certain holidays, Dec. 13-27.

THE ANDREW LOW HOUSE

—Drawing by Christopher Murphy

119 East Charlton Street: South side of Charlton Street opposite side of Colonial Dames House. Mr. Low's friend and associate, William Battersby, built this exceptional Barbados-styled home in 1852. Unique in Savannah, this type of architecture—with its unusual side entrance and walled garden—is often seen in Charleston. Frequently open to the public on spring tours, this house and its incomparable garden are rare treats for visitors.

123 East Charlton Street: Completed in 1969, this elegant reproduction follows in complete detail the typical Georgian structure of the 18th century.

Drivers and walkers finish circling the square, back to Abercorn and Harris Streets where the tour continues.

30. CATHEDRAL OF ST. JOHN THE BAPTIST: The oldest Roman Catholic church in Georgia and seat of the Diocese of Savannah. Organized in 1799, the congregation of St. John the Baptist erected its first house of worship on Liberty Square; in the 1830's a second, and larger, church was built on Drayton Street at Perry; and in 1876 the magnificent Victorian Gothic Cathedral was dedicated by Bishop William H. Gross—a zealous and indefatigable prelate who superintended the gigantic building task. After the cathedral was tragically destroyed by fire in 1898, rebuilding from the original design by architects Baldwin and Price was begun within the framework of the original walls.

The majesty of the stained glass windows and murals complete the unique splendor and beauty of the cathedral. With very few exceptions, all the windows were executed by Innsbruck Glassmakers in Austrian Tyrol and were installed around 1900. Visitors will wish to note, in addition to the impressive windows:

- The high altar of Italian marble
- The Chapel of the Sacred Heart
- The Chapel and Altar of the Blessed Virgin Mary
- The Stations of the Cross, imported from Munich
- The Coat of Arms of Pope John XXIII
- The Coat of Arms of Bishop Thomas J. McDonough
- The beautiful and detailed wall murals
- The Persian rugs, mainly Sarouks

—Drawing by Christopher Murphy

CATHEDRAL OF ST. JOHN THE BAPTIST

319 Abercorn Street: Across from the cathedral. Considered a notable example of its style, this brick house was built in 1888 for Fredericka Putzel and remodeled in 1895. During subsequent restoration, its original stucco was removed.

Continue north on Abercorn Street.

207 East Liberty Street: Southeast corner of Liberty and Abercorn Streets. The Sisters of Mercy, a convent which houses St. Vincent's Academy, was designed by Charles B. Cluskey and completed in 1845. With its beautiful iron gateways and fence, it is an appropriate adjunct to the cathedral complex.

The tour crosses Liberty Street, a tree-shaded avenue with charming old houses, many of them restored to their original elegance.

202-224 East Liberty Street: Northeast side of Liberty Street. Stretching for a full block to the east, this string of picturesque homes—built in the 1850s and 1860's—entices walkers to detour briefly for a closer view of yet another spectacular neighborhood in Old Savannah. At 212 East Liberty Street note the extraordinary ironwork.

31. COLONIAL PARK CEMETERY: East side of Abercorn Street. Opened about 1750 and closed to burials 100 years later, Colonial Cemetery was the second public burial ground in Old Savannah. Among the notable Georgians interred here were Button Gwinnett, a signer of the Declaration of Independence; Archibald Bulloch; James Habersham; Hugh McCall, Georgia's first historian; and Edward Green Malbone, the celebrated miniature painter. Visitors are welcome to explore the grounds and to examine the old tombstones and inscriptions.

By installing lights and a tabby sidewalk, repairing vaults and tombstones and providing extensive landscaping, the Trustees' Garden Club has restored the cemetery to its rightful beauty and dignity, establishing it as one of Savannah's most historic and beautiful restorations. Now tombstones and vaults are to undergo a further restoration and conservation program by the Savannah Park and Tree Department.

Drivers proceed on their tour by turning east on Oglethorpe Avenue, where Walk D begins at Landmark #32.

Walkers turn around at Oglethorpe Avenue, turning south to return to the starting point of Walk C, unless they want to combine Walks C and D (p. 64), in which case they also turn east on Oglethorpe Avenue to the start of Walk D.

217-219 Abercorn Street: West side of Abercorn across from cemetery. Constructed in 1872 as an apartment house, this handsome building has attractive dentil details over the windows and unusual cast iron balconies. It was built for Alfred Haywood from his own design.

124 East McDonough Street: Northwest corner of Abercorn and McDonough Streets. Built in 1861 by an unknown architect as a residence for Alfred Haywood, this imposing brick house with its delicate ironwork framing the entrance, the porch, and running around the second story, is one of Old Savannah's most exceptional structures. Its walled garden has a beautiful iron gate. Mr. Haywood, an Englishman from Oxford, came to Savannah a decade before the War Between the States and made a fortune by importing ice from the North. He held several offices of trust, serving as the first president of the city and suburban street railroad and as Chairman of the City Council.

231-233 Abercorn Street: Southwest corner of Abercorn and Perry Streets. With its interesting brick details which include segmental arches on the sides and brick quoins, this house was built in 1869.

120 East Liberty Street: Northwest corner of Liberty and Abercorn Streets. Note the gable roof, parapets and brick segmental arch windows heads of this house which was built in 1884.

125-129 East Liberty Street: Southwest corner of Liberty and Abercorn Streets. Converted into a mixed-use building, this house of the 1870's features twin iron balconies.

Walkers continue south on Abercorn Street, around Lafayette Square. Be sure to visit Landmark #29, the Colonial Dames House, (p. 69). Walk C ends at Jones and Abercorn Streets.

END OF WALK C

WALK D
"COLUMBIA SQUARE AND GREENE SQUARE RESTORATION"
(Walking Time: 1 to 1½ hours)

Drivers continue east on Oglethorpe Avenue along the northern boundary of Colonial Cemetery to Lincoln Street. If they wish, drivers may park by the cemetery and join walkers for a detour on foot which is inserted under Landmark #32. Otherwise, drivers may pick up their tour on page 77 at 204-216 East Oglethorpe (north side of the street).

Walkers begin on the southeast corner of Abercorn and Oglethorpe Avenue, walking east along Oglethorpe Avenue. Before beginning this tour, walkers may wish to read ahead for descriptions of a few outstanding houses which are well worth a short one-block detour west of the starting point of Walk D.

32. OGLETHORPE AVENUE: One of many Savannah streets which were originally designed with wooded center plats, Oglethorpe Avenue was the southern boundary of the colonial city and was called South Broad Street. Once a fashionable residential street, the avenue has regained its past distinction as the restoration and preservation of its captivating collection of old homes proceeds.

DETOUR FOR WALKERS
Walkers turn west on Oglethorpe Avenue for a one block detour which begins on the south side of the avenue.

113 East Oglethorpe Avenue: Located mid-block, this wood and stucco house with its airy two story porch is considered one of the city's finest buildings.

111 East Oglethorpe Avenue: Significant as a very good example of the 19th century Romantic domestic architecture, this quaint wood frame house with its jig-saw barge board remains intact as originally designed.

107 and 109 East Oglethorpe Avenue: Probably similar in design originally, these two houses were constructed about 1820 by and for Thomas Clark and Matthew Luftburrow. Both of these exceptional houses feature Flemish bond brickwork, high stoop entrances with brownstone steps and wrought iron railings, and doorways with elliptical arches, graceful columns and fan lights.

101-105 East Oglethorpe Avenue: Quite remarkable as examples of their style, these two houses, joined by a cast iron balustrade at the sidewalk, are similar in design—with the exception of their porticos, which were added sometime after their original construction about 1821-1822. Joseph E.

—Drawing by Ray Dilley

ROW HOUSE, OGLETHORPE AVENUE

Johnston, gallant Confederate general, was an insurance agent in Savannah after the War Between the States and lived at #105. Today a plaster bust, possibly Johnston, and other memorabilia of the Confederacy remain in this beautiful home.

Walkers now cross Oglethorpe Avenue to the north side and return to the start of Walk D by passing the following houses:

110 East Oglethorpe Avenue: North side of Oglethorpe Avenue, just east of Drayton Street. Popularly named the Lachlan McIntosh House for Revolutionary War General Lachlan McIntosh, one of its early visitors, this captivating old brick house—believed to be the oldest brick house in Georgia—was built about 1770 for use as a tavern by John Eppinger. Although the third story and ironwork were 19th century additions, the low stoop entrance, stone steps and floor, and transomed doorway remain as original "spectators" to the many historical events which transpired in this place of importance in early Savannah. Balls, public meetings and religious services were held here, and on these premises the first session of the Georgia Legislature was held. Today its elegant law offices aptly illustrate the Savannah practice of putting historic buildings to adaptive use—the pleasant pairing of residences and businesses which provides so much of the vitality of the Savannah Historic District.

112-114 East Oglethorpe Avenue: Notably fine architecture, about 1872, this pair of houses illustrates one of the practical uses of restoration—half being a residence and half a modern office.

116 East Oglethorpe Avenue: In 1869 when this fine brick dwelling was erected, the local paper cited it as "one of the most stylish structures" in the city. Its unusual bay window, which projects over the curved stairway, still distinguishes it today.

122 East Oglethorpe Avenue: Endearing for its modesty and understatement, this charming house has been a favorite study for authorities of 18th century architecture who credit the wooden story and a half to the mid-1700's. It was raised on a brick foundation in 1871. Two small dormer windows break the steep line of the roof of the clapboard dwelling and a small wood railed balcony makes the front ornate. Sheltering one of Savannah's loveliest gardens, the house is a treasured tribute to early Georgia.

END OF DETOUR

Walk D now begins officially. Walker's may remain on the north side of Oglethorpe Avenue for a close view of the homes or they may return to the south side (as the map shows) for a view which offers a better perspective.

Drivers continue east on the south side of Oglethorpe Avenue.

204-216, 220 and 224 East Oglethorpe Avenue: Beginning at the northeast corner of Oglethorpe and Abercorn, these notable 19th century row houses are high stooped and iron bedecked in the tradition of their enduring style.

228 East Oglethorpe Avenue: Mid-block. Adjoining famous Marshall Row, this house was built in 1855. Note brick work, dentil trim, ironwork, doorways, and triple windows.

230-244 East Oglethorpe Avenue: Completing the block to Lincoln Street. Marshall Row, as the next four Savannah gray brick buildings are named, was built in 1855-56. Well-deserved are the national accolades bestowed upon its architecture—which has been ably restored. The pattern of the brick work is basic American bond. High stoops with the original marble steps accentuated by wrought ironwork, wide doors with brass doorknobs, and the details at the roof line are an expression of the dignity of its style. Note earthquake bolts at #244.

Drivers and walkers turn north on Lincoln Street. In turning, note the fine view of the rear of the Marshall Row buildings.

140 Lincoln Street: Across the street, northeast corner of Lincoln Street and the lane. Remaining as an excellent example of early 19th century wood frame architecture, this dwelling features the thick wide board siding which is in such demand for restoration today. It was built about 1813.

134 Lincoln Street: Next door. Its famous six-over-nine windows provide unusual interest to this frame house. Constructed at the turn of the 19th century (?), this federal style house exhibits a classic portico, modified gable roof line, as well as a more recent whimsical dolphin downspout and fine wrought iron garden gate around the corner.

Continue north on Lincoln Street, crossing East York Street.

127-131 Lincoln Street: Northwest corner of Lincoln and York Streets. These fine paired houses were built about 1855 and were rented to prominent Savannahians. The northern house (with a street address at 227 East President Street) was the home of Judge William Law, eminent lawyer and jurist; the southern house (with a street address at 228 East York Street) was the home of General Alexander R. Lawton, Confederate officer, lawyer and American charge d'affaires to the Court of Vienna. During his last visit to Savannah in 1870, Robert E. Lee paid a call here to General and Mrs. Lawton. The complex was restored in 1986 and now houses an Inn.

1790 Inn and Restaurant: Southeast corner of Lincoln and President Streets. Valued as one of the few late Federal houses remaining in Savannah, this clapboard house was built between 1820-1824, and, as it is restored and used today, offers the visitor multiple attractions. Housing elegant guest rooms and a restaurant highlighted by original flagstone flooring, wide beams and antique furnishings—all cozily reminiscent of Old England, the house affords an irresistible old world atmosphere to those who like to combine dining out with architectural sleuthing. In addition to the original Adams mantels, ceilings and molding which enhance this house is the unique interior construction—very likely a forerunner of our present pre-fab constructions: clapboards which have been exposed in the kitchen area reveal studs and joists which were mortised systematically by matching Roman numerals! The adjacent building was built c. 1888 and is now part of the inn.

The tour turns east on President Street and enters Columbia Square.

33. COLUMBIA SQUARE: The tour partially circles Columbia Square to the other part of East President Street where it continues east. Named as a testimonial to the poetic title of the new United States, Columbia Square was laid out in 1799. The Davenport House, its dominant feature, will be described later on the tour. When Savannah was a walled city from 1757-1790, one of the six city gates, Bethesda gate, was located here. Much of the Northeast quadrant of the city, which was spared destruction by the fires which periodically ravaged Savannah, is notable for a preponderance of wooden structures dating from the earliest days of the city.

Heineman House: 125 Habersham Street, on the west side of the square between President and York Streets. This notable stucco over brick mansion was built in 1842. It is now being restored to a single family house after many years as an apartment house.

Sheftall House: 321 East York Street, southwest corner of York and Habersham Streets. Considered a rarity in Savannah, both for its excellent architectural style and its age, early 19th century. It is an example of an early frame dwelling, with a central chimney, hip roof and unique front door fanlight. The basement was added later. The Sheftall House was carefully relocated on this corner—where is stands as a tribute to one of the city's oldest and most civic-minded families.

136 Habersham Street: Across the street, southeast corner of Habersham and York Streets. One of Savannah's most valuable wood frame houses, this building was constructed before 1809 by Frederick Ball, master carpenter of Savannah. Its gable roof and wide board siding are particularly notable. It has been beautifully restored recently and now has a lovely garden. Note distinguished neighboring houses, recently restored.

130 Habersham Street: Northeast corner of Habersham and York Streets. Constructed in 1885. Notice beautiful wrought iron galleries and gracious, full length windows.

128 Habersham Street: Southeast corner of Habersham and President Streets. With its fine brick parapet and cornice dentils, this building has been remodelled in keeping with its original design of the 1850's.

Turn east on President Street.

425 East President Street: Note one of the rare successful examples of modern architecture in the historic district, incorporating the details, motifs and scale of its older neighbors.

424 East President Street: Northwest corner of Price and President Streets. Remaining as another good example of wood frame construction

with a gable roof, this house was built in 1810.

503 East President Street: Southeast corner of President and Price Streets. Featuring a high pitch gable roof, gable dormers and chimneys, this exceptional wood frame house was built before 1809.

509 East President Street: This picturesque, compact cottage, built before 1808, is a style unique in the city. Its "second half" is at 510 East York Street.

The tour enters Greene Square.

34. GREENE SQUARE: Laid out in 1799, Greene Square was named for Revolutionary War hero Nathanael Greene who died near Savannah and is buried beneath the huge monument in Johnson Square.

The tour circles Greene Square.

On many of the streets which skirt the square are house markers which record the original colonial street names as they were before they were changed after the Revolutionary War. Today's President Street was King Street, after the Monarch of England; State Street was Prince Street, after the Prince of Wales; and Congress Street (two blocks north) was Duke Street, after the Duke of York.

As the tour rounds the southwest corner of the square, several delightful restorations will beckon walkers a few steps west of the route on York Street.

The 500 block of York Street is the largest example of skillful architecture in houses built by free Blacks.

510 East York Street: This is the second half to 509 East President Street, perhaps once a single block-wide house. Built before 1816, it is reputed to have a well hidden beneath its wide-board floor.

513 East York Street: Across the street. This wood frame house is valued for its many 19th century features: high pitch gable roof and wide board siding. It was built in 1853.

131 Houston Street: Northwest corner of Houston and York Streets. A gingerbread structure of late Victorian design, this house, with its wedding cake design, has joined the ranks of Savannah's fascinating fun-restorations. Built in the 19th century, its Victorian elements were added in the late 20th century.

521 East York Street: Southwest corner of Houston and York Streets, where tour rounds the square. This handsome residence was built in the mid-19th century and displays to perfection the famous Savannah gray bricks

—Drawing by Christopher Murphy

SKYLINE

from the old Hermitage Plantation. Tabby mortar (limestone and oyster shells) was used to place the bricks. The skillful modern addition from 1978 is not visible from the square and thus preserves the historic appearance.

124 Houston Street: Northeast corner of Houston and President Streets. An early 19th century wood frame house with a stucco basement, this building has been extensively remodeled.

542 East State Street: As the tour turns into State Street, this fine wood frame house appears to the right. Built about 1800, its gable roof and dormer windows make it a distinctive example of early architecture. It was raised on a brick foundation in the mid-19th century.

536 East State Street: Just off Houston Street. This diminutive residence was built in 1845 for Mr. John Dorsett. Note the Fire Department medallions here on the chimney, also next door and on several other area houses. These markers identified the patrons of the early fire brigade; non-subscribers would witness the loss of their burning houses.

117-119 Houston Street: Northwest corner of Houston and State Streets. Continuing on State Street, the tour passes this attractive restoration of the early 19th century, the first home of the Savannah Female Orphanage.

Second African Baptist Church: On the west side of the square, rising between State and President Streets, the Second African Baptist Church stands on the site where it was organized on Dec. 26, 1802, with twenty-six members. It is the second oldest, colored Baptist Church in North America and had its origins in the baptism of Andrew Bryan (p. 29). In this church some say that General William T. Sherman issued the famous Field Order #15, granting the newly freed slave "40 acres and a mule." Completely rebuilt after a fire in 1925, the church contains its original pulpit, prayer benches and choir chairs.

The tour continues west on State Street.

520 East State Street: This two story frame house offers a fine example of the Savannah stoop: wrought iron balcony, Savannah gray brick and paving stone steps.

514-516 East State Street: Lillibridge II, standing three stories with a gambrel roof, dormers and central chimney, and The Cottage, with its square bay window and ornamental chimney, are exact replicas of two houses built by Hampton Lillibridge in the 18th century.

502-512 East State Street: Anderson Row, built about 1890, is an excellent brick restoration with an eye-catching display of doorways and iron balconies.

The tour continues west on State Street across Price Street.

422-424 East State Street: Northwest corner of Price and State Streets. Considered to be among Savannah's finest paired houses, these brick buildings are excellent examples of mid-19th century two story brick residences.

Laura's House: Next door at 420 East State Street. Named for its former long term tenant, Mrs. Laura Jones, this unpretentious frame house was built between 1799 and 1809. Known as a Davenport tenement, it was illustrated in **The Early Architecture of Georgia.** It was saved by Historic Savannah Foundation and authentically restored by a fine lady after it was moved from another location. The entire house is original heart pine. It has basically two rooms, with a freestanding fireplace which is the focal point for the living-dining room.

It is sheltered by the Bonticou Double House, a two story clapboard house, with wide weathered boards on the exterior and outstanding interior wood details. It was built after 1853 and also moved from its former location.

—Photo by Van Jones Martin

THE ISAIAH DAVENPORT HOUSE

(83)

402 East State Street: Northeast corner of State and Habersham Streets. Francis Stone, an alderman in pre-Civil War days who was commended for his valuable services during the yellow fever epidemic of 1854, built this house about 1820. The two story clapboard house over a brick basement with a high stoop is a fine example of early 19th century Savannah architecture. Note its unusual 6 over 9 window placement.

35. **DAVENPORT HOUSE:** Northwest corner of State and Habersham Streets. The rich architectural detail of the interior of this elegant quintessential Federal style house is a delightful surprise to the visitor who has first been oriented to its simple exterior of English brick. Built in 1820 by master builder Isaiah Davenport for himself, this dignified mansion ranks among the great quintessential Federal style houses of America. Destined for demolition in 1955, it was saved by a group of outraged Savannah Society ladies who raised $22,500 to buy the Davenport House and who established Historic Savannah Foundation (p. 90). Restored as a handsome museum, it features very fine woodwork and plasterwork. Chippendale, Hepplewhite and Sheraton furniture and a superior collection of Davenport china highlight its long list of attributes.

Enhancing its attraction is the charming garden of 18th century design, created by the Trustees' Garden Club as its bicentennial project. House and garden are open Mon.-Sat. 10:00 to 4:30; Sun., 1:30 to 4:00. In the basement is Historic Savannah's Museum Shop, featuring specialty items unique to Savannah and Isaiah's time period. All proceeds from the Museum Shop support Historic Savannah Foundation's preservation projects.

Kehoe House: 123 Habersham Street, on the west side of Columbia Square. This Queen Anne Victorian house was built as a single family house in 1893 by W. Kehoe, a foundry owner. The dark red brick mansion is surrounded with balconies, porches, ironwork and handrailings. Note the cast iron cornice. After standing vacant for almost ten years it was beautifully restored as an inn.

Continue west on President Street.

36. **RICHARDSON-OWENS-THOMAS HOUSE:** Stretching the depth of a full block, the Richardson-Owens-Thomas House faces Oglethorpe Square on Abercorn Street and is bordered by Lincoln Street at the rear; the tour route, going west down President Street, affords an excellent view of the entire property—the carriage house, garden and mansion.

One of America's magnificent examples of the English Regency Period, designed by William Jay and built during 1816-1819, this mansion is distinguished as an architectural treasure by its columned entrance portico, winding double stairway, paneled parapet above the main cornice, arched second story windows and rare interior design. Note the grandeur of the decor and the furnishings. As an added attraction, the entire lower floor—with its superbly furnished kitchen, laundry room, wine cellar and larder—

—Painting by Leonora Quarterman

RICHARDSON-OWENS-THOMAS HOUSE

have been restored. Visiting here on his American Tour in March, 1825, the Marquis de Lafayette spoke from the south balcony. Open Sunday and Monday, 2:00 to 5:00; other days, 10:00 to 5:00.

Cluskey Building: 127-129 Abercorn Street, across the square between York and President Streets. Built in 1859 as excellent examples of rental property of the highest quality—a distinction their restored offices and apartments enjoy today—these Classical Revival structures are simply designed with brick, brownstone and ironwork in artful combination.

END OF WALK D

Drivers turn north to round the corner of Oglethorpe Square to State Street, where they turn west to Bull Street, to view Landmark #37, the Lutheran Church of the Ascension (p. 46), and further north on Bull Street to Landmark #38, Christ Episcopal Church (p. 44), where the tour ends. If drivers have visited these sites earlier on their tour (p. 44), this marks the end of the driving tour.

Extra Dividends

Outstanding historic buildings off the tour route—but easy to find.

The Champion, Harper-Fowlkes House
Savannah, Georgia

Yolanda Fiorentino Schofield
©...anno domini 1988....

CHAMPION, HARPER-FOWLKES HOUSE

The Cottage Shop: 2422 Abercorn Street. In this quaint antebellum plantation cottage, with its distinctive gallery, is now one of Savannah's finest gift shops. Built by John Maupas in 1848, it stood on his mother's share of the extensive Drouillard Plantation.

123 West Oglethorpe Avenue: This perfectly restored Federal style house, constructed in 1822 by Samuel Bryant, was moved from across the street. It originally stood on an early land grant, given to Giles Becu in 1734, by King George II. Of particular interest are the arched opening above the door which encases a fan light, dormer windows, brick cornices, brick lintels above the windows, brownstone sills and brownstone paving on the stoop.

Champion, Harper-Fowlkes House: 230 Barnard Street. As Savannah's outstanding example of the fully developed Greek Revival style, this superb house is attributed to architect Charles B. Cluskey. It was built in 1844 for Aaron Champion.

In 1939 Alida Harper Fowlkes purchased the house and furnished it with priceless antiques. It was bequeathed in 1985 to the Society of the Cincinnati in the State of Georgia.

Facing Orleans Square, it has a dramatic entrance formed by imposing iron gates, double curved sandstone steps and four Corinthian-type columns two stories high. The entrance hall, floored with black and white marble, has four square columns surrounding an oval rotunda through which a sky light is seen three stories above. At present, it is open to the public for special tours only.

The King-Tisdell Cottage: 514 East Huntingdon Street. The King-Tisdell Cottage is the preservation triumph of a very successful community cooperative effort. The City of Savannah donated the cottage and funds for its resettlement and renovation; Historic Savannah Foundation donated the land and professional restoration services to the Beach Institute Neighborhood Association; and the Association for the Study of Afro-American Life and History volunteered to operate the cottage as a museum that preserves Savannah's black history and culture.

Built in 1896 by W.W. Aimar on another site, the cottage is significant for its unusually intricate gingerbread ornamentation of the porch and dormers in a style employing wheels and spindles. The museum displays art objects,

—Drawing by Rick Spitzmiller

THE KING-TISDELL COTTAGE

documents relating to black history and furniture appropriate to a coastal black residence of the 1890's. Open Mon.-Fri., 12:00-4:30 p.m., Sat.-Sun., 1:00-4:30 p.m. King-Tisdell Cottage Black History Museum and the King-Tisdell Cottage Foundation sponsor the excellent "Negro Heritage Trail" Tour. For information call 234-8000.

Beach Institute: 502 East Harris Street. Built in 1865 by teachers of the American Missionary Association it was the first school for blacks and became a public school in 1919. Currently the Beach Institute is an African-American Cultural Center which features very interesting exhibitions. Open Mon.-Fri. noon-5 p.m., Sat.-Sun. 1 p.m.-5 p.m. Phone 234-8000.

Price Street Row Houses: Savannah is not only home of Georgia's oldest African-American community but also of one of the most historically significant African-American communities in the nation. The Price Street Row Houses from #422 to #504 are the heart of the oldest Black neighborhood in downtown Savannah.

The Victorian District

Gingerbread Is Beautiful! Drive through the Victorian District—bounded by East Broad, Martin Luther King, Jr., Blvd., Gwinnett and Anderson Streets—just south of the Historic District. Victorian District tours are offered. For information contact the Visitors Center, 944-0456 . Architectural signatures of the period—stained glass windows, lively gingerbread trim and imaginative shapes and details—will delight you at every turn. Note p. 138.

The Victorian District is a 45 block, 162 acre area which was named to the National Register of Historic Places in 1974. Late 19th century two-story homes of wood frame on brick foundations characterize the district—Savannah's first suburb.

Originally populated by middle class families, the neighborhood had deteriorated severely by 1974 when a non-profit housing corporation, Savannah Landmark Rehabilitation Project, committed itself to rehabilitating substandard rental units for low-income residents, to ensuring social and economic diversity, and to avoiding the displacement of the present tenants. Supported by public and private financing, the SLRP's rehabilitation program was visibly successful throughout the Victorian District.

Historic Savannah Foundation

Historic Savannah Foundation is a private, non-profit membership organization dedicated to preserving Savannah's architectural heritage and unique city plan, advocating compatible new development, educating the public in preservation principles and techniques, and enhancing the livability of Savannah's historic districts. Today the Foundation keeps vigil over the National Landmark Historic District and Victorian District and provides advice and technical assistance to other local historic areas.

Established in 1955, when a few concerned citizens saved the historic Isaiah Davenport House from demolition, the Foundation remains a true leader in the field of historic preservation. Its Revolving Fund, devised to enable HSF to purchase endangered buildings and resell them for private restoration, has been a model for the nation. The Foundation itself has restored two buildings, the Davenport House (p. 84) and the William Scarbrough House (p. 29).

The Foundation has an active educational program, coordinating the annual Georgia Heritage Celebration, co-sponsoring the annual Tour of Homes, and sponsoring an annual lecture series. HSF offers a Special Tours service to special-interest groups wishing to visit Savannah and has published four instructive and entertaining books.

Committed to the sensitive revitalization of the entire urban area, HSF strives to promote responsible new development as well as authentic restorations. Through its ward-by-ward survey, the Foundation identified many "quality of life" issues and is working with residents and city officials to assure neighborhood livability. After focusing on residential renovation in the Historic District, where over 1,100 architecturally significant structures have been preserved since 1955, HSF has turned its attention to promoting the revitalization of the historic downtown area—a commitment demonstrated by locating its offices at 212 West Broughton Street.

Four Forts

From the moment of her birth, when she constructed fortifications against the Spanish and the Indians, Savannah has upheld an honorable record of military tradition which is evidenced by the rolls of honor so proudly cherished in her churches and immortalized by four of her most historic forts. These, along with their museums of relics and artifacts, have been opened to the public.

Steeped in battle history, Savannah is a rich resource for annalists of America's military past, and visits to four of her famous forts recreate the drama of some of Georgia's major conflicts. Forts Pulaski, Screven and Jackson are all featured in Excursion III. Fort McAllister may be reached by a short detour from U.S. #17 South, as described in Trip No. 2.

FORT JACKSON: Restored as an important link in the fort chain along the Savannah River, Fort Jackson is a handsome brick fortification, the offspring of a Revolutionary War battery which was bought by the federal government in 1808; garrisoned during the War of 1812; rebuilt in 1842; and occupied by Confederates during the War Between the States. The fort, with its Maritime Museum and Black Military History Museum, which features actual uniforms, weapons and instruments and traces the impact of Blacks during the civil war, is open daily 9:00-5:00. Special tours for children, students, seniors, and adults. Lunch and dinner programs are available, which include historic presentations, cannon firings and meals.

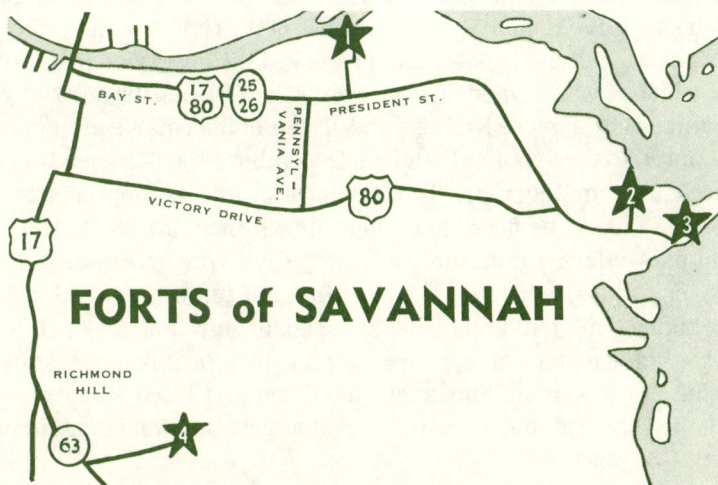

FORTS of SAVANNAH

FORT PULASKI: Named for that gallant Pole, Gen. Casimir Pulaski who lost his life in the unsuccessful siege of Savannah in 1779, Fort Pulaski was built between 1829 and the mid-1840's on Cockspur Island to guard the sea-approach to Savannah. Its towering walls, wide draw-bridge and two moats recapture the past when the fortress was considered impregnable. Among the engineers who raised its massive ramparts was young Robert E. Lee, West Point graduate. Occupied by Confederate troops in 1861, the fort fell to Union forces in April, 1862, when they overcame it with rifled cannon, the first used in warfare. Fort Pulaski was proclaimed a National Monument in 1924, was restored and is now operated by the U.S. Park Service.

John Wesley, founder of Methodism, landed in America in 1736 at Cockspur Island. A monument to him is a short distance from the fort.

Along the park trails notice the variety of plant and animal life on the island. Picnic area.

Hours: Daily except Dec. 25, 8:30 a.m.-5:00 p.m. and until 6:45 p.m. during the summer. For further information call 786-5787.

FORT SCREVEN: Built about 1875, Fort Screven was manned during the Spanish-American War, World War I and World War II—when General George C. Marshall commanded it. This modern beach fort, never actually restored, captivates visitors who marvel at private residences nestled atop its walls, its magnificent view of the Atlantic and the Savannah River, and the panorama of local history which its museum depicts. Not restored. Next to Tybee Museum (p. 107).

FORT McALLISTER STATE HISTORIC PARK: Located on the south bank of the Great Ogeechee River, Fort McAllister is an outstanding example of Confederate earthwork fortifications. Built in 1861-1862 to guard the "back door" to Savannah, it denied the use of the river to Union vessels; protected a vital railroad trestle; and preserved the river rice plantations (for one of which it was named) from Union raids. During 1862-1863 it repulsed seven attacks by armored vessels and, as one of Sherman's major objectives in his March to the Sea, finally fell on December 13, 1864, when Union forces captured it from the rear. The earthworks and bombproofs have been restored as closely as possible to their appearance in 1863-64. The beautiful coastal park offers a museum containing Civil War artifacts. Audio-visual shows for groups, educational programs and tours are available. Picnic areas, hiking trail, tent and trailer sites, boat ramps and dock. Different annual special events. Park hours: 7 a.m.-10 p.m.; historic sites hours: Tues.-Sat. 9 a.m.-5 p.m., Sun. 2:30 p.m.-5:30 p.m. Closed Mon. (except legal holidays), Thanksgiving, Christmas. For reservations and more information call (912) 727-2339.

Highways and Byways

Only by exploring the highways and byways skirting Savannah can the visitor grasp the scope of the historical heritage of the Savannah coastal area where the marshes and rivers frame points of interest noted for their antiquity, charm and unspoiled beauty. Each of the following excursions highlights attractions located on the following Area Map; each may be visited in one to four hours, allowing the visitor leisure for browsing, photographing and strolling.

ARDSLEY PARK-CHATHAM CRESCENT

On the way to Excursion I (page 97) the visitor will enjoy a brief detour to the Ardsley Park-Chatham Crescent suburb which is bounded by Victory Drive, Bull Street, Waters Avenue and 54th Street. Baldwin Park, a portion of Chatham Crescent, extends north of Victory Drive.

The two residential garden neighborhoods may best be seen by walking or driving at random through the gracious tree-lined streets, which are interrupted by shaded squares (reminiscent of Oglethorpe's plan) in Ardsley Park and by circles, a formal mall and a landscaped crescent design (attributed to the Beaux Arts and City Beautiful movements) in Chatham Crescent. Built between 1910 and 1930, during an era of prosperity, both subdivisions feature large lots, terraced lawns, and early 20th century eclectic and revival architecture. Using hundreds of shade trees, lot owners landscaped broad expanses of lawns along the streetscape, forming a community of scenery unobstructed by walls.

Follow Whitaker Street South to Victory Drive; turn east on Victory Drive to Bull Street; turn south on Bull Street to Washington Avenue. Turn east on Washington Avenue, one of Savannah's most beautiful streets, which lies between 46th and 48th Streets. Travel beneath its canopy of oak trees for several blocks until the mall at Atlantic Avenue appears to the left. Turn north and circle the mall back to Washington Avenue. Then strike out on your own to explore this gracious suburb where Spanish castles, Italian villas, Greek mansions and Gothic castles line the streets. Continuously preserved by its long-term residents and protected by deed restrictions, this idyllic suburb is listed as an historic district on the National Register of Historic Places. Return to Victory Drive via Washington Avenue and Bull Street to begin Excursion I.

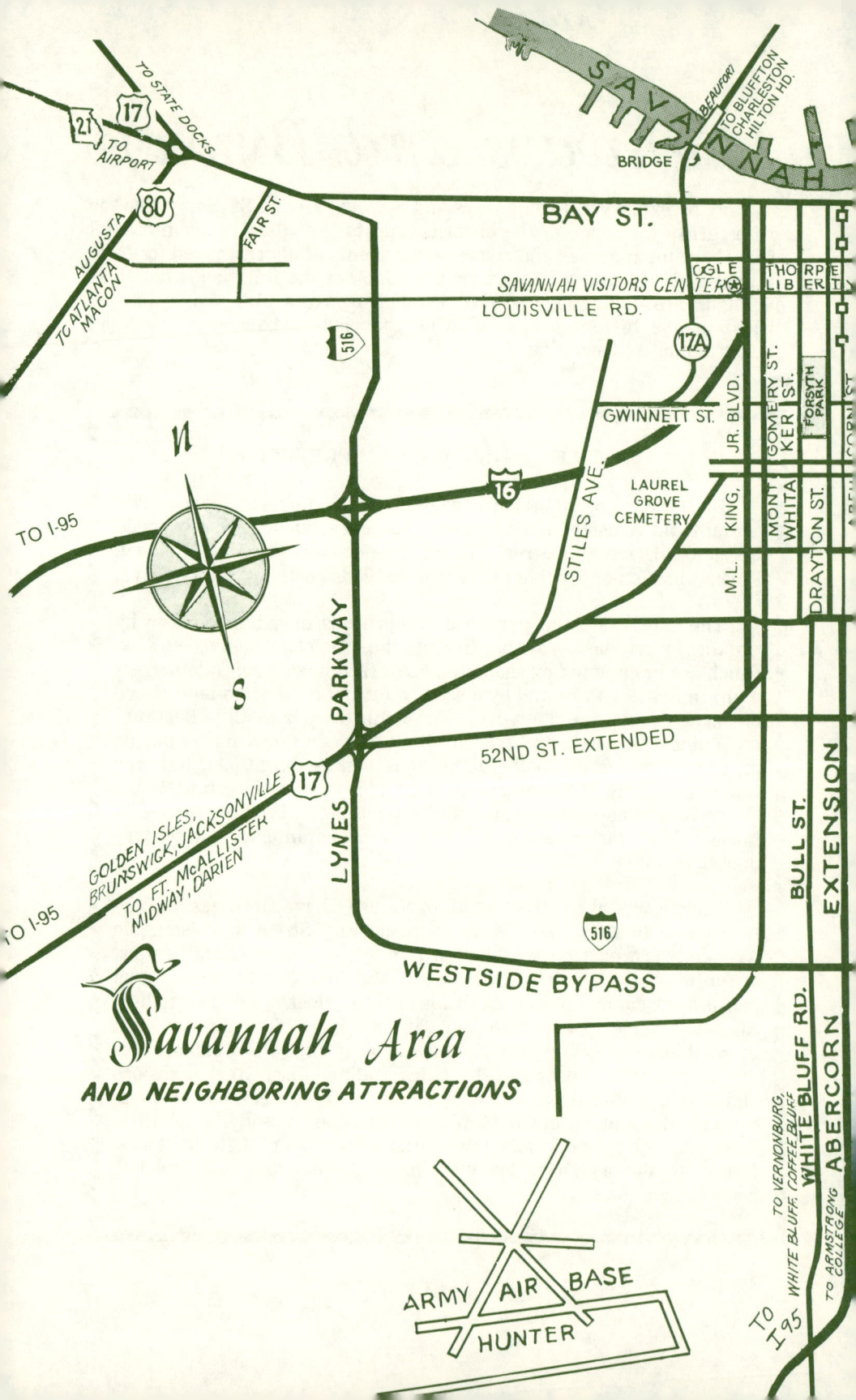

TO STATE DOCKS

27 17 TO STATE DOCKS

TO AIRPORT

80

AUGUSTA

TO ATLANTA MACON

FAIR ST.

516

TO I-95

N

S

PARKWAY

17

LYNES

GOLDEN ISLES, BRUNSWICK, JACKSONVILLE

TO FT. McALLISTER MIDWAY, DARIEN

TO I-95

SAVANNAH

BRIDGE

TO BLUFFTON CHARLESTON HILTON HD.

BEAUFORT

BAY ST.

SAVANNAH VISITORS CENTER

LOUISVILLE RD.

OGLE THORPE LIB RP IER

17A

GWINNETT ST.

16

STILES AVE.

LAUREL GROVE CEMETERY

JR. BLVD.

MONTGOMERY ST.

KER ST.

FORSYTH PARK

WHIT

DRAYTON ST.

M.L. KING,

MONT WHITA

52ND ST. EXTENDED

516

WESTSIDE BYPASS

BULL ST.

EXTENSION

ABERCORN

WHITE BLUFF RD.

TO VERNONBURG, WHITE BLUFF, COFFEE BLUFF

TO ARMSTRONG COLLEGE

TO I-95

𝓢avannah Area
AND NEIGHBORING ATTRACTIONS

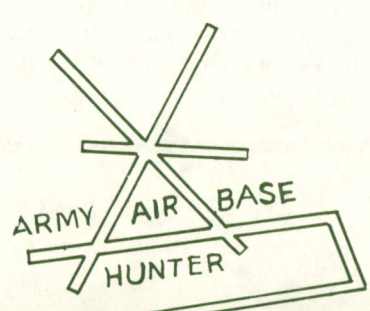

ARMY AIR BASE
HUNTER

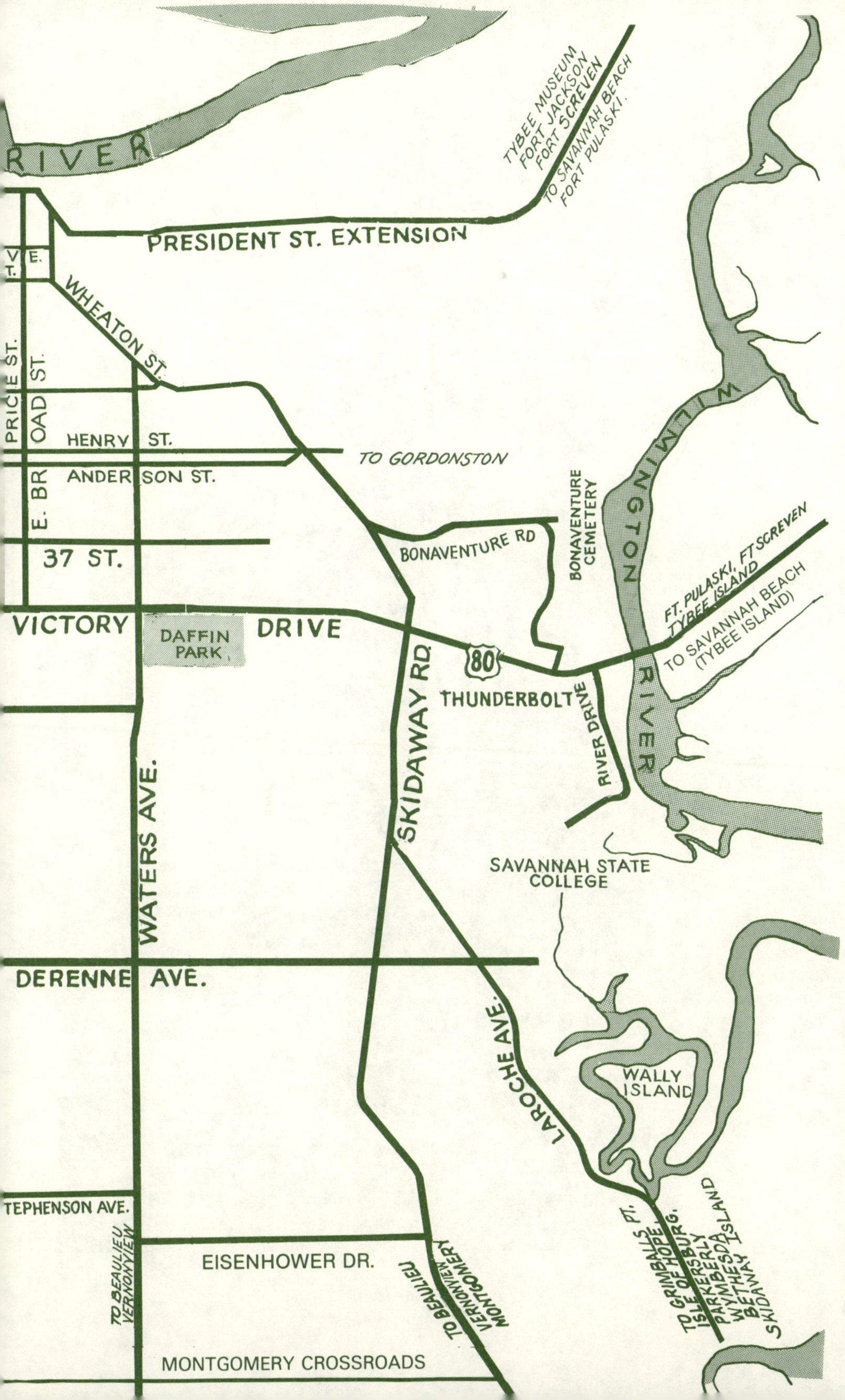
RIVER
TYBEE MUSEUM
FORT JACKSON
FORT SCREVEN
TO SAVANNAH BEACH
FORT PULASKI.
PRESIDENT ST. EXTENSION
WHEATON ST.
PRICE ST.
E. BROAD ST.
HENRY ST.
ANDERSON ST.
TO GORDONSTON
37 ST.
BONAVENTURE RD
BONAVENTURE CEMETERY
WILMINGTON RIVER
FT. PULASKI, FT SCREVEN
TYBEE ISLAND
TO SAVANNAH BEACH
(TYBEE ISLAND)
VICTORY
DRIVE
DAFFIN PARK
80
SKIDAWAY RD.
THUNDERBOLT
RIVER DRIVE
SAVANNAH STATE COLLEGE
WATERS AVE.
DERENNE AVE.
LAROCHE AVE.
WALLY ISLAND
TEPHENSON AVE.
EISENHOWER DR.
TO BEAULIEU VERNONVIEW
TO BEAULIEU VERNONVIEW MONTGOMERY
TO GRIMBALLS PT. ISLE OF HOPE ISLE OF BURG. PARKERSBY WYMBESDA BETHWAY ISLAND SKIDAWAY
MONTGOMERY CROSSROADS

L. Quarterman -

SHRIMP BOATS AT THUNDERBOLT

—Painting by Leonora Quarterman

EXCURSION I

BONAVENTURE - THUNDERBOLT

(Driving Time: About 2 hours)

VICTORY DRIVE: Points of interest in Excursion I may be reached by going east on Victory Drive, an extension of U.S. Highway 80. Victory Drive, a memorial to the servicemen of World War I, is one of Savannah's most spectacular streets—world-famous for its three miles of imposing palms, lavish azaleas and stately mansions. An eye appealing focal point on historic Victory Drive are the two spectacular floating fountains in the Daffin Park lake featuring jets of water shooting 60 feet into the air. The fountains, a project by the Rotary Clubs for the beautification of Savannah, are lit by night. The drive ends at the Wilmington River where Excursion I continues to Thunderbolt.

THUNDERBOLT: To reach Thunderbolt, turn right on River Drive, just before the bridge over the Wilmington River. Originally an old Indian village, Thunderbolt derives its name from an old tradition which tells of a bolt of lightning that struck here, causing a spring of clear water to gush forth. Picturesque and profitable, the quaint harbor is the center of Savannah's shrimp industry, whose workers in late afternoon bustle to and from the laden shrimp boats tied at dockside. Yachts and colorful small craft crowd these waters, many of them following the inland waterway between the North and Florida. In the distance to the east rises the Sheraton Savannah Resort.

SAVANNAH STATE COLLEGE: To reach Savannah State College follow River Drive as it curves west to become Falligant Avenue; continue to College Street where the campus begins. Founded in 1890, it was the first publicly supported state college for the education and training of black students in Georgia. Savannah State College, sometimes called the "College by the Sea," is an important institution serving several thousand students who profit from a modern curriculum housed in gracious old buildings in a tranquil, traditional setting.

"DAISY'S GATES"

L. Quarterman
—Painting by Leonora Quarterman

BONAVENTURE CEMETERY: Return to River Drive and follow it north across Victory Drive to Mechanics Avenue, which is the left hand road at the fork, where it becomes Bonaventure Road. As the road curves sharply west, turn right, into the cemetery gates. Open from dawn until dusk, Bonaventure Cemetery is guarded by 200 year old live oaks which trail their mosses over the graves of many of Savannah's heroic statesmen, citizens and soldiers. Originally the home of Colonel Mulryne, Bonaventure became the plantation home of Mary, Colonel Mulryne's daughter, and her husband, Josiah Tattnell, in 1760. The property was cherished by their descendants until it was sold in 1847 for use as a cemetery. Luxurious with camellias, wisteria, azaleas and yellow jasmine, and canopied by magnolia, live oak and dogwood trees, Bonaventure is a paradise of natural beauty, one of the nation's most photographed river front gardens.

GORDONSTON AND "DAISY'S GATES": Follow the Bonaventure Road west from the cemetery gates and continue to Skidaway Road; follow Skidaway north past the gates of Gordonston to Egdewood Road; turn right and follow Edgewood Road to the iron-fenced Girl Scout Memorial Park. Originally the site of a farm owned by the family of William Washington Gordon II, Gordonston became one of Savannah's most pleasant garden suburbs when it was subdivided in the 1920's.

Bordered by Edgewood Road and Gordonston Avenue, the Girl Scout Memorial Park was left to the children of Savannah by Juliette Gordon Low, founder of the Girl Scouts of America. Set in the Edgewood Road section of the park's fence are side panels from the celebrated "Daisy's gates," creative masterpieces by Juliette "Daisy" Low who personally designed, fired and hand-wrought their ironwork for her English estate. The gates themselves have been removed to the garden of the Juliette Gordon Low birthplace. (See page 50.)

Return to the city via Skidaway Road.

END OF EXCURSION I

Say you saw it in "Sojourn in Savannah!"

EXCURSION II

SUBURBS ON THE MARSHES

(Driving Time: About ½ day)

No experience quite matches the delight of driving along the salt rivers and marshes where the suburban communities of Grimball's Point, Isle of Hope, Beaulieu, Vernon View, White Bluff and Coffee Bluff have assembled some of Savannah's most beautiful homes and gardens in an idyllic setting of unspoiled natural beauty.

The tour follows Victory Drive east to Skidaway Road, turns right and follows Skidaway Road to LaRoche Avenue where it winds left at Savannah State College, following the route where once the famous American Grand Prize and Vanderbilt Cup Automobile races were held. LaRoche turns left via Hopecrest Avenue through Parkersburg, once a large plantation, and intersects with the Grimball Point Road, a full left turn. Just before Dutch Island, Grimball Point Road bears right.

GRIMBALL'S POINT: (about 3 mi.) Surrounded by beautiful gardens of azaleas and oaks, the private homes at Grimball's Point adorn one of Savannah's most secluded waterfront sites where winding lanes assure its residents pastoral privacy.

ISLE OF HOPE: (½ mi.) Return to LaRoche Avenue, turn left and follow it south into Bluff Road which continues south, tracing the Isle of Hope.
On the high shell bluff are built dignified old houses with fascinating histories, several of them dating from the early 1800's when they were used as summer homes. Isle of Hope is listed as an historic district on the National Register of Historic Places.

WORMSLOE PLANTATION: (just under 1 mi.) Bluff Road turns sharp right and leads to the Avenue of Pines, the first left turn. Follow it to Richmond Drive and turn right; Wormsloe's fenced park and then its imposing entrance will appear to the left.
Constructed by Noble Jones, one of Georgia's first settlers who came to Savannah with Oglethorpe aboard the ship Anne in 1733, the 500 acres of Wormsloe were first leased from the Trustees of the Colony of Georgia in 1733, and later received into the family by a Royal Grant in 1756, and remained as the only Savannah plantation in the possession of its original owners until 1973, when the property was acquired by the State of Georgia through the Nature Conservancy. The family retained the house, library and surrounding gardens. Noble Jones, commanding a company of marines and charged with Georgia's coastal defense, constructed a fortified house at Wormsloe between 1739 and 1745. This defensive post was designed to protect

the inland water approach to Savannah from the south against Spanish attacks. Wormsloe also aided Savannah during both the Revolution and the War Between the States. Remains of this fort, built of tabby, still guard the river. The fort was abandoned when the Jones family built the present home north of the site in 1828. In addition to its loyal defense of the colony, the Jones family is noted for its contributions to the medical, cultural and civic life of the community, and, as testimony to its unexcelled collections of rare Georgia documents and manuscripts—which are now housed by the University of Georgia—a classic marble library stands near the three story mansion in a garden unequaled anywhere in the South. Live oak drive, public grounds, museum, interpretive area, nature trail and fort ruins. Call 353-3023. Open Tues.-Sat., 9:00-5:00; Sun., 2:00-5:30. Closed Monday.

BETHESDA: (2 miles) Exit Wormsloe and turn left on Richmond Road which intersects the Parkersburg Road, which becomes Skidaway Road right at Wormsloe. Follow Skidaway Road west through Wymberly, now a subdivided plantation, to Ferguson Avenue. Turn left and continue south to Bethesda whose dairy farm fence appears to the left and leads to the entrance.

The first Bethesda was founded in 1740 by the Reverend George Whitefield, the present Bethesda by the Union Society in the second half of the 19th century. It provides today, as a home for boys, educational, vocational and cultural programs whose graduates are men of fine character and ability. The home suffered serious setbacks from 1770 until 1867, being twice destroyed by fire and removed to various other locations for temporary periods. The present building was built in 1855 by the Union Society, trustees of Bethesda, and has been continuously occupied since 1867. Set in a fine sweep of land, Bethesda is a natural beauty spot, enhanced by a lovely chapel, the Whitefield Memorial which was erected by the Georgia Society

BETHESDA HOME FOR BOYS
Old engraving before later changes

of Colonial Dames of America in 1925; by an outdoor water-front theater, the gift of the Trustees Garden Club; and by the Cunningham Historic Center. Open Mon.-Fri., 9:00-5:00.

SKIDAWAY ISLAND: Upon leaving Bethesda turn left on Ferguson Avenue. At Diamond Causeway, turn left toward Skidaway Island, which attracts with its state park, oceanography center and numerous good quality golf courses. People from all parts of the United States retire to a beautifully landscaped, private development on the island.

SKIDAWAY ISLAND STATE PARK: Having both salt and fresh water due to estuaries and marshes that flow through the area, this park is a barrier island. During the summer months nature programs are offered, which also can be arranged in the off season. There are two nature trails, a picnic area, camping facilities, a playground and a Jr. Olympic swimming pool. Park hours: 7 a.m.-10 p.m. Picnic area is open till sunset. For information call 598-2300.

AQUARIUM: As a part of the Marine Extension Service of the University of Georgia, the Aquarium exhibits over 200 live animals representing approximately 50 species of fish and invertebrates. It features exhibitions about the historical and prehistorical uses of coastal resources and about the Gray's Reef National Marine Sanctuary. Open weekdays 8 a.m.-4 p.m., Sat., 12 p.m.-5 p.m. Tours are available by reservation in advance. For information call 598-FISH.

Leave Skidaway Island via Diamond Causeway, continuing to its intersection with Ferguson Avenue.

VERNON VIEW: (about 3 mi.) Turn left on Ferguson Avenue, turn left on Shipyard Road, and follow it across the marshes to Vernon View which begins at Center Street/Drive on Burnside Island. Continue on Center Drive into McAlpin Street; turn left on McAlpin and left again on Cushing; then turn left on Sullivan which completes the circle through Vernon View back to Center Street. At Center Street, turn right on Shipyard Road to continue the tour.

Overlooking the Burnside River, nearby its neighbor Rio Vista on the Moon River, Vernon View is a charming little community whose homes on the high bluff command an excellent view of the inland waterway between New York and Florida.

BEAULIEU: (nearly 2 mi.; pronounced "Beyoo-lee") Retrace Shipyard Road, going west into Beaulieu Avenue; turn left and follow the curves of Beaulieu Avenue past Beaulieu's estates, turning right at Whitfield Avenue. If you turn left there lies Montgomery, with some beautiful old houses on a beautiful old road.

The road through Beaulieu leads behind the homes, affording only occasional glimpses of the Vernon River on whose grassy banks Count d'Estaing landed his forces in 1779 during the Revolution. Civil War batteries were also erected here. First settled as the plantation home of William Stephens, Beaulieu later became a summer resort and today is shared by year-round residents who maintain beautifully landscaped estates.

VERNONBURG AND WHITE BLUFF: (about 7½ mi.) After driving through Beaulieu, continue on Whitfield Avenue and bear left where Whitfield Avenue intersects Diamond Causeway and continue north on it for 4 miles, passing Halcyon Bluff, to Montgomery Crossroads. (Visitors who wish to interrupt the tour by a detour back to town may leave the tour by turning left on Montgomery Crossroads and returning to town via any of the main city streets which bisect it.) Turn left on Montgomery Crossroads, drive 1.1 miles and turn left again on the White Bluff Road (an extension of historic Bull Street.) Follow it south for 2 miles to Davidson Avenue. Turn left and follow Davidson to Rockwell Avenue; turn right and then right again at Vernonburg Avenue, returning to White Bluff Road.

Settled in 1742 by German-Swiss immigrants, the town of Vernonburg was located at White Bluff on the wandering banks of the Vernon River. Originally hoping to practice the art of silk culture, the settlers discovered however that the soil was best used for planting cotton and thus Vernonburg became the cradle of Georgia's cotton planting and manufacturing of cotton cloth. Incorporated since 1866, it is Chatham County's smallest town—where suburban families have established riverfront retreats where boating, crabbing, and swimming provide rural relaxation just as they did in colonial days.

From White Bluff, turn left at the historical marker for Nicholsonboro onto the Old Coffee Bluff Road to visit Nicholsonville and its churches.

NICHOLSONBORO BAPTIST CHURCH: The church was founded in 1868 by freed slaves mainly from St. Catherine's Island. In 1882, 18 members of the Nicholsonville community paid off a $5000 mortgage to obtain the title for the land upon which the Nicholsonboro churches now stand. Probably about that time the first church on this site was built. With the prospering of the community the present Nicholsonboro Baptist Church was built in 1890. Both of the churches possess architectural significance since they are important examples of rural Negro church construction of the late 19th century in South Georgia. Only very few survived from this period. Both are rectangular frame buildings with gabled tin roofs surmounted by small wooden steeples.

Circle back to White Bluff Road past a beautiful panoramic marsh view.

COFFEE BLUFF: (3 mi.) Turn left and follow White Bluff Road into its extension, Coffee Bluff Road, going south to the Forest River. Stop here for a refreshment break on the river bank. Then turn west to the Carmelite Monastery on West Back Street (unpaved) and circle back to the Coffee Bluff Road.

Coffee Bluff is part of Rose Dhu Island and was formerly laid out as a park. The bluff was probably named for John Coffee, a colonial landowner who lived near Midway.

The Carmelite Monastery is a cloistered order of nuns who withdrew from the public in 1958. Phone 925-8505 to see the chapel.

The tour returns to the city by retracing Coffee Bluff—White Bluff Road, going north past Oglethorpe Mall, one of Savannah's two shopping malls. Hunter Army Air Field lies along White Bluff Road, beginning at Montgomery Crossroads.

ARMSTRONG STATE COLLEGE: (about 4½ mi.) Those who wish to see Armstrong State College may detour left off White Bluff Road, after about 3 miles, into Holland Road which intersects the Abercorn Extension. Turn left on Abercorn Extension and follow it south to the college.

Armstrong State College began in 1935 as Armstrong Junior College, situated in the old Armstrong home on Bull Street (p. 61); in 1964 it became a four-year institution and in 1965 moved to its present new campus.

Opposite of the College is the Savannah Mall, the city's newest mall.

To return to the city follow Abercorn Extension north.

END OF EXCURSION II

EXCURSION III

TYBEE ISLAND

(Driving Time: 2 to 3 hours)

A round-trip excursion to Tybee, an Indian word meaning "salt," is especially appealing to families with children who will enjoy the forts and museums en route to the island, the expanse of beach—which is Georgia's summertime playground—and the fishing and boating accommodations which are available along the rivers that weave through the marshes between Tybee and Savannah. Although a cursory trip may be made in less than two hours, many families choose Tybee for an all-day jaunt—complete with swimming, picnicking, sightseeing and exploring. Motels, cottages, rental houses and seafood restaurants provide bed and board for those interested in a longer visit.

Tybee Island may be reached by two convenient routes, each providing its own attractions. It is suggested that newcomers follow Victory Drive, an extension of U.S. Highway 80 (see Excursion I), to the Wilmington River where the first bridge on the Tybee Road begins. The return trip from the island may be made over the Islands Expressway, which intersects the Tybee Road mid-way between the island and Savannah and ends, via President Street Extension, in downtown Savannah.

WHITEMARSH AND WILMINGTON ISLANDS: The Tybee Road crosses Whitemarsh and Wilmington Islands, both thickly wooded sanctuaries favored by summer and year-round residents who are drawn to the unspoiled terrain, wonderful waterways and the history of the desperate conflicts fought here during the War Between the States. Side trips to the interiors of these islands may be made by brief detours on various side roads which intersect the Tybee Road.

Of special interest is the Sheraton Savannah Resort Inn and Country Club, whose imposing elegance and spectacular golf course command one of the most splendid sites on Wilmington Island. To reach it, turn right on the Wilmington Island Road which intersects the Tybee Road.

NATURE TRAIL: On the way to Tybee Island, a three mile multipurpose nature trail follows the bed of the abandoned Tybee Railroad from just east of the Bull River Bridge to Elba Creek. From Savannah take U.S. Highway 80 East until it crosses the Bull River Bridge, just east of Wilmington Island. The path is perfect for hiking, cycling and picnicking in a lush, natural environment where different animals habitant to this area, such as turtles, opossum, rabbits, and the occasional alligator, might be seen.

MOSSY OAK ON THE MARSH

—Painting by Leonora Quarterman

FORT PULASKI (p. 92): Fort Pulaski National Monument can be seen on the left just before the Tybee Road reaches Tybee Island.

TYBEE ISLAND, SAVANNAH BEACH: Nostalgically remembered is the rollicking railroad which once connected the mainland to Savannah Beach whose multiple attractions have lured Savannahians and "landlubbers" for generations. Here, it can be said, there is something for all: fishing, crabbing, boating, surfing in specially designated areas, swimming, beachcombing and picnicking in Memorial Park. The Library is open to all who wish to browse, rest or read. Variety stores and galleries offer an array of goods from all over the world, an amusement park, a water slide and a miniature golf park provide entertainment for the whole family, and a museum, an old fort and the Marine Science Center offer educational opportunities.

FORT SCREVEN (p. 92): Note signs after entering Tybee Island. The intriguing remains of Fort Screven, one of the last Atlantic coastal forts, now fascinate amateur archeologists, "diggers" and "climbers" of all ages.

TYBEE LIGHTHOUSE: General James Oglethorpe, the founder of Savannah, ordered the construction of a lighthouse on Tybee Island. The original tower, built in 1736, was soon destroyed by a storm. The present 154 foot structure was built in the second half of the 18th century and is still a beacon to Savannah sailors and provides an endurance test for those wishing to climb for the view. The lighthouse is located at Fort Screven.

TYBEE MUSEUM: At Fort Screven, artifacts, displays and relics of pre-Colonial and Colonial days are arranged along winding tunnels, once the fort's batteries. The lighthouse and the museum are open Apr.-Sept. daily 10 a.m.-6 p.m., closed Tues., Oct.-Mar. Mon., Wed., Thurs., Fri., noon-4 p.m., Sat., Sun. 10 a.m.-4 p.m. Closed Tues., Thanksgiving, Christmas and New Year's. For information call 786-5801.

TYBEE ISLAND MARINE SCIENCE CENTER: Between 15th and 16th Streets on the Strand. Between Memorial Day and Labor Day the center offers "discovery walks," beach walks where the participants learn about the formation of the beach and examine animals living on the beach and in the sea. Visitors are also encouraged to visit the exhibitions at the center. During the summer every Saturday night the center sponsors lectures about the marine and coastal environment. Special children programs are offered (p. 125). Open Wed.-Sun. 9 a.m.-5 p.m. Check times before your visit! For more information call 786-5917.

FORT JACKSON (p. 91): To visit Fort Jackson on the return trip, follow the Islands Expressway, which becomes President Street Extension, and turn north at the fort sign. Especially interesting are the moat and exhibits.

END OF EXCURSION III

Farther Afield

Clustered to the north and the south are close relatives of Savannah—sea island shareholders in her coastal history, topography, low country beauty and cultural heritage. Cloistered and unspoiled, these communities offer visitors an unsurpassable variety of waterfront and historic attractions which may be enjoyed either on day trips or overnight journeys. Restaurants and motels are available.

—By Elizabeth O'Neill Verner

Bluffton, Beaufort, Hilton Head

TRIP No. 1

(Driving Time: Round Trip, Savannah, full day)

SAVANNAH NATIONAL WILDLIFE REFUGE: On the way to these lovely old places visitors may wish to make a small detour to visit the excellent Savannah National Wildlife Refuge to have a closer look at coastal Georgia's sensitive ecosystem. More than 26,000 acres of land offer exotic birds, alligators and other animals habitant to this area. Take U.S. Highway #17 North (not U.S. Highway #17 A) from Savannah. Accessible by car. Open: From sunrise to sunset. Phone: 652-4415.

The shortest route to nearby South Carolina resorts is U.S. #17A which crosses the Savannah River via the "New Savannah Bridge," which as of this printing does not have an official name. This incredible bridge, which is 2039 feet long and 417 feet high, and is a new monument in Savannah, was recently completed to replace the Eugene Talmadge Memorial Bridge since the latter was not tall enough for the modern ships.

If visitors come from the National Wildlife Refuge continue on U.S. Highway #17 North.

Bluffton, Beaufort and Hilton Head are closely linked and may be visited in one long day, as Trip No. 1 describes, or they may be seen singly on shorter drives of a few hours each—with perhaps an overnight stop scheduled in between. A South Carolina road map will indicate the best route depending upon time and interests.

BLUFFTON: (24 miles from Savannah) Turn right off of U.S. #17 onto S.C. #170 and right again onto S.C. #46. A quaint old village on the May River, Bluffton is the tranquil home of "summer people" and those in retirement. The Church of the Cross, a handsome Gothic cruciform building completed in 1857, is a favorite of artists, historians and all those who seek the secrets of this serene settlement.

HILTON HEAD: (39 miles from Savannah) After driving through Bluffton, continue east on S.C. #46 to U.S. Highway #278 to Hilton Head Island, one of the nation's most celebrated golf, tennis, and beach resorts.

Hilton Head is a year-round resort equipped to handle both conventions and family groups (who love the supervised children's programs!) Fine oceanfront resorts, inns and cottages are located in the midst of a host of outdoor activities, which include everything from golf on numerous courses to fishing, bird shooting, tennis, birdwatching and beachcombing.

BEAUFORT: (42 miles from Savannah) From Hilton Head follow U.S. #278. Turn north at its junction with S.C. #170 and follow #170 to Beaufort. Lavish with landmarks from four centuries of history, Beaufort is one of the South's most charming mixtures of past and present. The Beaufort area was explored by the Spanish in 1514, settled briefly by French Huguenots in 1562, colonized by the Scotch Covenators in 1613 and finally claimed by the English in 1663. The town of Beaufort was chartered in 1712 and survived the Revolutionary War and the Civil War with a flourishing economy built on indigo, rice and cotton.

As spokesmen for this era of prosperity, beautiful old homes line the waterfront areas—one of the most enchanting walking tours in the South. Sight-seeing maps, listing historic sites and landmarks, are available. Annual Water Festival in July.

FRIPP ISLAND: Drive seaward on S.C. #21. As a newcomer to the roster of sea island resorts which provide the best in accommodations and seaside sports in an unspoiled coastal setting, Fripp Island offers an ocean front inn and an 18-hole golf course for those who wish to island hop as they golf.

OTHER BEAUFORT BONUSES: Other side trips out of Beaufort may be planned with the Beaufort Chamber of Commerce. Favorites are Sheldon Church (c. 1746), Parris Island (U.S. Marine barracks and recruiting depot), Hunting Island State Park, Lady's Island and St. Helena's Island.

Midway and the Golden Isles

TRIP No. 2

(Driving Time: Round Trip, Savannah, full day)

Follow I-16 to I-95 South for 81 miles—cross the beautifully wooded Ogeechee River; past historic plantations, modern farms and once prosperous rice fields; over the famed Marshes of Glynn to the Golden Isles—a chain of romantic islands joined to the city of Brunswick by causeways. Although it is possible to hit the high spots of this wonderful trip in one day, the attractions are so numerous and the lodgings on the Golden Isles so inviting that an overnight trip—or longer—is suggested.

FORT McALLISTER (p. 92): Just east of Richmond Hill, where Henry Ford bought an old plantation for a winter home, Fort McAllister is a worthwhile detour.

MIDWAY: (30 miles from Savannah) Uniquely patriotic with a history which echos one of America's most imposing roll calls of outstanding ministers, statesmen, generals, scholars and scientists, Midway—with its quaint old church and adjacent museum—has an "historical pedigree" unexcelled in our country. First built in 1756, Midway Church was rebuilt in 1792. With its tiny graveyard it stands today as a tribute to its many sons and daughters who helped to shape the destiny of this nation. Visit the old church with its large slave gallery and high pulpit, study its old gravestones, whose inscriptions read like a veritable Who's Who of colonial times, and browse through the Midway Museum, which displays furnished rooms, documents and exhibits. Open 10:00-4:00 Tues.-Sat.; 2:00-4:00 Sun.; closed on Mon. and holidays.

—Painting by Leonora Quarterman

OLD MIDWAY CHURCH

DARIEN: (61 miles from Savannah) Settled by Oglethorpe on Georgia's frontier in 1735 to protect the infant colony from the Spanish were the Scottish Highlanders who founded the little town of Darien. Close by the courthouse is a huge old live oak, so enormous that it is said to have sheltered an entire company of Oglethorpe's soldiers.

THE MARSHES OF GLYNN: Lying between Darien and Brunswick are the Marshes of Glynn, today a State Wild Life Refuge. Georgia's greatest poet, Sidney Lanier, immortalized the incomparable scene by his best loved poem "The Marshes of Glynn."

BRUNSWICK: (81 miles from Savannah) Founded in 1771, the busy port of Brunswick is the gateway to the Golden Isles. A powerful industrial community, Brunswick is noted for its turpentine, rosin, creosote and related commodities. Especially oriented to the needs of visitors, Brunswick's Welcome Center is a gracious host to those wishing information about island accommodations, sightseeing and transportation.

THE GOLDEN ISLES: Beautifully developed for modern living—both private and resort—the Golden Isles offer a kaleidoscope of pleasures in almost every area of entertainment. As a group, their historic sagas fill volumes, and their individual attributes set them aside as paradise islands— each to be enjoyed in its own way. Before crossing the bridges to the islands study detailed brochures about their attractions and accommodations.

ST. SIMONS ISLAND: Heavily wooded St. Simons has been under the flags of Spain, France, England, the U.S. and the Confederate States of America. Near Fort Frederica (open to the public) Oglethorpe defeated the Spanish in the famed Battle of the Bloody Marsh; both John and Charles Wesley served as rectors of Christ Church at Frederica. On the south shore is a well-equipped beach resort which offers golf as well as favorite beach-side activities. Museum of Coastal History.

SEA ISLAND: Dotted with many beautiful small estates and popularized by its large excellent hotel, Sea Island is world famous as a luxury resort beloved by golfers and lovers of uncommercialized seaside pursuits.

—Painting by Leonora Quarterman

LIGHTHOUSE ON ST. SIMONS ISLAND

JEKYLL ISLAND: For sixty years millionaires such as the Goulds, Morgans, Cranes and Rockefellers owned Jekyll Island, using it as a winter hideaway. Purchased by the State of Georgia and operated as a State park, Jekyll Island today is one of the nation's finest family and convention resorts. A new dimension is added to swimming by Jekyll's Aquarama, part of a multi-million dollar convention facility; hiking, camping, museum trips, golf, tours of millionaire mansions and a sightseeing train are special features of a versatile vacation agenda.

To return to Savannah, retrace I-95 to I-16; or, to continue to Jacksonville, follow I-95 south.

END OF TRIP No. 2

Ebenezer and Jerusalem Lutheran Church

TRIP No. 3

(Driving Time: Round Trip, Savannah, one hour)

Follow Ga. #21 northwest for 14 miles to Rincon; continue on #21 for three more miles to its junction with Ga. #275; turn right and follow #275 for about five miles. At the Savannah River the road winds to an end at the Jerusalem Lutheran Church, which, with one restored house, is all that remains of the colonial village of Ebenezer. Founded in 1736 by a group of Salzburger exiles, Ebenezer once boasted 500 people, 160 town lots, market squares, a flour mill and a pulp mill. Today the Georgia Salzburger Society has established a museum where you may see evidence of Salzburger history attractively displayed. Built in 1767 to 1769, the quaint church, the oldest standing church in Georgia, is constructed of bricks made from local clay. It has held regular services for over 200 years.

END OF TRIP No. 3

Olympic Games 1996

Savannah will join Atlanta and Athens as hosts of the Summer Olympic Games in 1996. The yachting competitions will be in the Atlantic Ocean just off the coast of Savannah, near Tybee Island. Competitions are held in eight or ten boat classes and the number of competitors is limited to 450. Boats running in these events are rather small, ranging from 11'0" to 26'11", quite a bit smaller than those competing in the America's Cup.

The Olympic marina is planned for Priest's Landing on Skidaway Island. Fans can watch the competitions from Tybee Island, Savannah's beach, or from Little Tybee or Warsaw Island, both of which are undeveloped and accessible only by boat.

All the other sports events will take place in Atlanta and Athens, about 256 miles (400 km) from Savannah. A regular shuttle service between Atlanta and Savannah is planned.

Numerous sports and cultural events and festivals in Savannah, across Georgia and the region will precede and accompany the sports events. A four-year Cultural Olympiad will present a series of multi-disciplinary festivals showcasing the arts and cultures of more than a dozen nations. The Cultural Olympiad culminates in a nine-week festival in the summer of 1996.

For further information please contact Savannah Olympic Support Council, 428 Bull Street, Savannah, Georgia 31401 U.S.A., (912) 231-1996.

Cultural Scene

Savannah is a very lively city from a cultural point of view. The famous Savannah Symphony and two very good theater companies entertain throughout the season. An active jazz community presents good jazz to a knowledgeable and enthusiastic audience. The wonderful museums and house museums enrich everyone's cultural and scientific life, while scores of festivals and parades bring fun for the whole family.

Thanks to a remarkable public-private partnership, Savannah is one of the cities with the biggest exposure to unique cultural events in the nation. Cultural life is made possible by the efforts and strong support of countless friends and dedicated volunteers.

In addition to these suggestions for "what to do in Savannah," contact the "artsline" of the city of Savannah, which offers a recording of current information about cultural events. Telephone 233-ARTS, or contact the Savannah Visitors Center, 944-0456, or see the entertainment section of the newspaper.

Theaters and Dance

Savannah Theatre Company: 222 Bull St. (p. 53), Box office: 222 Bull Street, 233-7764.

The Savannah Theatre Company is housed in the oldest continuously operating theater in the United States. It opened on Dec. 4, 1818. During its days as a playhouse some of the greatest dramatic and operatic stars performed here.

The current Savannah Theatre Company was incorporated in May, 1950, as the Little Theatre of Savannah, Inc. In 1981 the Little Theatre purchased the historic Savannah Theatre and changed the company's name to The Savannah Theatre Company, Inc., to match the historic theater it now occupies. The Savannah Theatre Company produces 7 to 12 plays and musicals yearly.

City Lights Theater Company: 125 East Broughton Street, Box Office: 234-9860.

City Lights Theater Company was founded in 1981 as a non-profit community theater company. In addition to its regular season, City Lights produces an annual playwrighting competition that concludes each year with the Savannah playwright's festival. Very popular is the annual Shakespeare in the Park Festival. The company was recently rated number six in the State by the Georgia Council for the Arts.

City Lights Theater recently moved into its new location at 125 East Broughton St., where the city's new theater district is developing with the restoration of the Lucas Theatre, the City Lights Theater and the Weis Theater.

Lucas Theatre: On the corner of Abercorn and Congress Streets (p. 41).

On December 26, 1921, Arthur Lucas welcomed patrons to the pride and joy of his movie theater chain. It was hailed as the most handsome movie theater in the South, one of Georgia's architectural treasures. The Lucas was designed to house silent films and vaudeville shows. However, with the advent of talkies in the early thirties, the theater became exclusively a movie house where three generations of Savannahians experienced entertainment in the grand style. The Lucas was "the" place to go on a special date, and gentlemen were not admitted without a jacket and tie.

In 1976 the Lucas fell victim to the suburban migration and closed. Spurred by several threats that the theater be demolished, a group of citizens formed a non-profit organization dedicated to restoring this irreplaceable structure as closely as possible to its former grandeur. The Lucas Theatre for the Arts, Inc., purchased the building in 1989 and is currently raising the funds to put the Lucas back into operation. When it reopens, the theater will host performing arts events, such as concerts, opera, dance, films, and lectures, as well as corporate and convention meetings, civic activities and private parties and receptions. For further information call 232-1696.

For performance information on **commercial live theaters**, see the entertainment section of the newspaper.

Savannah has two **Ballet companies** which produce several performances yearly. Consult the daily newspaper or call 233-ARTS for performance dates.

Musical Activities

Savannah Symphony Orchestra:
The Savannah Symphony Orchestra, established in 1953 by Chauncey Kelly as a community orchestra, is now the largest performing arts organization in Georgia outside of metropolitan Atlanta. With a core of 37 full-time musicians, the Savannah Symphony presents over 250 performances each year in its 9-month season, from September through May. Its high calibre attracts such world-class artists as Itzhak Perlman, Pinchas Zuckerman, Midori and Yo-Yo Ma. Performances are broadcast state-wide on Georgia Public Television and Peach State Public Radio. Performances range from full-orchestra Masterworks to chamber orchestra concerts to ensemble recitals to Pops extravaganzas. Very popular also are the open air performances in parks and on River Street.
For concert schedules and tickets call the Symphony office at 236-9536.

Savannah Onstage:
This annual music festival features performances by outstanding young artists, all winners of coveted top prizes from the world's prestigious music competitions. The festival is held in February or March. To make reservations, receive a brochure or find out about travel packages call: 236-5745 or 1-800-CLAVIER.

Jazz:
Savannah's roots in Jazz run long and deep. The city, like other older and established southern communities, has a long-identified African American population, and with that population has come the art form popularly known as Jazz.
Probably the genesis of Savannah Jazz was in the life and culture of old

West Broad Street, now Martin Luther King, Jr., Blvd. The sights, the sites, the sounds of West Broad Street are now part of our collective historical legacy, but long ago it was the nexus of community life for African Americans. Clubs, sporting places, diners, and theaters all abounded there, and they produced the sounds and exponents of Savannah Jazz.

A review of the Savannah Jazz Hall of Fame, which is at the museum of the Coastal Jazz Association in City Market, will richly attest to the city's claim as a major generator of top-flight talent. On the walls of that museum are the biographies and pictures of such personages as Joe "King" Oliver, the mentor of Louis Armstrong; "Jabbo" Smith, one of the most advanced trumpeters of his days and a rival to the great Satchmo; and lyricist, songwriter and singer Johnny Mercer, who wrote over 1500 songs which are today a treasury of the songwriter's art.

Today, Jazz remains alive and vibrant in Savannah. One of the great American Jazz Festivals falls annually in September, bringing international talent before thousands of people from all over the world. The city's special ambiance is also reflected in several great clubs which are helping to forge a Savannah Jazz renaissance.

Concerts in Johnson Square:
Savannah's leading series of outdoor music performances in a historic square is held every Wednesday and Friday from 11:30 a.m. to 1:30 p.m. through the months of June, July and August. These free, two hour lunchtime concerts feature the music - jazz, dance band, and Dixieland - of some of Savannah's finest professional musicians.

Museums

Beach Institute: (p. 88) African-American Culture Center, 502 East Harris St., 234-8000, Mon.-Fri. Noon-5 p.m., Sat.-Sun. 1 p.m.-5 p.m.

City Market Art Center: (p. 30) at Jefferson and West St. Julian St., 232-4903, Mon.-Sat. 10 p.m.-6 p.m., Sun. 1 p.m.-5 p.m.

Coastal Jazz Hall of Fame and Museum: (p. 30, 117) 207 West St. Julian St. in City Market, 232-2222, Mon.-Fri. 10 a.m.-5 p.m.

Davenport House Museum (p. 84) 324 East State Street, 236-8097, Mon.-Sat. 10 a.m.-4:30 p.m., Sun. 1:30 p.m.-4 p.m., closed on major holidays; last tour begins at 4 p.m.

Fort McAllister Historic Park: (p. 92) 394-A Fort McAllister Road, Richmond Hill, Ga. 31324, (912) 727-2339. Park hours: 7 a.m.-10 p.m.; historic site hours Tues.-Sat., 9 a.m.-5 p.m., Sun. 2 p.m.-5:30 p.m. closed Mon. except legal holidays, Thanksgiving, Christmas.

Fort Pulaski National Monument: (p. 92) U.S. Highway 80 E., 786-5787, summer daily 8:30 a.m.-6:45 p.m., winter 8:30 a.m.-5 p.m., closed Christmas.

Georgia Roundhouse Complex: (p. 27) 601 West Harris St., 238-1779, Mon. through Sat. 10 a.m. to 4 p.m., Sun. 12 noon to 4 p.m., guided tours daily 1 p.m.

The Green-Meldrim House: (p. 55) 327 Bull St., Tues., Thurs., Fri., Sat. 10 a.m.-4 p.m., closed Dec. 15-Jan. 15, 2 weeks prior to Easter.

The Hamilton-Turner House Museum: (p. 68) 330 Abercorn St.

King Tisdell Cottage, Black History Museum: (p. 87) 514 East Huntington St., 234-8000, Mon.-Fri. 12 noon-4:30 p.m., Sat., Sun. 1 p.m.-4:30 p.m.

The Andrew Low House Museum: (p. 69) 329 Abercorn St., 233-6854, weekdays 10:30 a.m.-4 p.m., Sun. 12 p.m.-4 p.m., closed Thurs., certain holidays, Dec. 13-27, last tour at 4 p.m.

Juliette Gordon Low Girl Scout National Center (p. 50) 142 Bull St., 233-4501, Mon.-Sat. 10 a.m.-4 p.m., Sun. 12:30 p.m.-4:30 p.m., closed Wed., Sun. in Dec. and Jan. and major holidays.

Old Fort Jackson: (p. 91) 1 Ft. Jackson Rd., 232-3945, daily 9 a.m.-5 p.m., July 1-Aug. 15 until 7 p.m. Costumed military programs.

The Richardson-Owens-Thomas House Museum (p. 84) 124 Abercorn St., 233-9743, Tues.-Sat. 10 a.m.-5 p.m., Sun. and Mon. 2 p.m.-5 p.m., closed major holidays and Jan., last guided tour 4:30.

River Street Train Museum: (p. 32) 315 West River St., 233-6175, Mon.-Sat. 11 a.m.-5:30 p.m., Sun. 1 p.m.-6 p.m.

Savannah History Museum (p. 27) 303 Martin Luther King, Jr., Blvd., 238-1779, daily 9 a.m.-5 p.m.

Savannah Science Museum: (p. 123) 4405 Paulsen St., 355-6705, Tues.-Sat. 10 a.m.-5 p.m., Sun. 2 p.m.-5 p.m., closed Mon. Children's program, p. 123.

Ships of the Sea Museum: (p. 32) 503 East River St., 232-1511, open daily 10 a.m.-5 p.m.

Skidaway Marine Science Complex, Aquarium: (p. 102) north end of Skidaway Island, 598-FISH, weekdays 8 a.m.-4 p.m., Sat. 12 noon-5 p.m.

Telfair Academy of Arts and Sciences, Historic House and Art Gallery,

Savannah's Art Museum: (p. 48) 121 Barnard St., 232-1177, Tues.-Sat. 10 a.m.-5 p.m., Sun., 2 p.m.-5 p.m., closed Mon. and all major holidays. Children's program, p. 123.

Tybee Island Lighthouse: (p. 107) 30 Meddin Dr., Tybee Island, 786-5801, Apr.-Sept. 10 a.m.-6 p.m., Oct.-Mar. weekdays 12 noon-4 p.m., Sat.-Sun., 10 a.m.-4 p.m., closed Tues., Thanksgiving, Christmas, New Year's Day.

Tybee Island Marine Science Center: (p. 107) 1510 Strand, Tybee Island, 786-5917, Children's program, p. 125.

Tybee Museum/Fort Screven: (p. 107) 30 Meddin Dr., Tybee Island, 786-4077, Apr.-Sept. daily 10 a.m.-6 p.m.; Oct.-Mar. Mon., Wed., Thurs., Fri., 12 noon-4 p.m., Sat. and Sun. 10 a.m.-4 p.m., closed Tues., Thanksgiving, Christmas and New Year.

Wormsloe State Historic Site: (p. 100) 7601 Skidaway Rd., 353-3023, Tues.-Sat. 9 a.m.-5 p.m., Sun. 2 p.m.-5:30 p.m., closed Mon. (exception some legal holidays), Thanksgiving, Christmas.

College Activities

Armstrong State College: 11935 Abercorn St., 927-5325; plays, lectures, concerts, and chamber music.

Savannah State College: Thunderbolt, Ga., 356-2248; concerts, drama and fine arts series.

Savannah College of Art and Design: 342 Bull St., 238-2400 or via Artsline 233-ARTS; Art exhibitions, plays and films.

Festivals

Savannah is by all means a festival city. Almost every week you will find Savannahians celebrating something in the loveliest places in town. For more information call the Artsline, 233-ARTS, or the Visitors Center, 944-0456.

An overview of the highlights throughout the year:

First Saturday Festival: Every first Saturday of the month 10 a.m.-5 p.m., Rousakis Plaza, River St. Entertainment, sidewalk flea markets and handicraft markets, food.

February:

Georgia Heritage Celebration: begins about Feb. 1 and runs for nearly two weeks. Commemorates founding of Georgia. Tours, art exhibits, craft demonstrations. Includes Super Museum Sunday (free admission to most museums); Sponsored by the Historic Savannah Foundation and the Chatham County Board of Education. Telephone 233-7787.

Savannah Onstage: (p. 116) Telephone 236-5745.

March:

St. Patrick's Day Parade: March 17, 10 a.m., one of the biggest celebrations of that day in the country.

Tour of Homes and Gardens: Candlelight and day tours of historic private homes and gardens. For information and tickets call 234-8054. Sponsored by Christ Episcopal Church and Historic Savannah Foundation.

April:

Hidden Gardens of the NOGS Tour: Walking tour of hidden gardens in the historic part of Savannah "north of Gaston Street." Telephone 238-0248.

A Night in Old Savannah: 3 evening fun and food festival. Downtown Savannah. Ethnic food booths. Constant entertainment. Jazz.

May:

Arts on the River Festival: Visual and performing arts festival on River Street. Concerts. Food. Open air concert at the river with the Savannah Symphony Orchestra.

July:

Forsyth Festival: Festival in Forsyth Park downtown. Music, dance, theater.

Great American 4th of July: Entertainment, arts and crafts, fireworks on River Street.

September:

The Savannah Maritime Festival: Festival in connection with the Olympic Games.

Savannah Jazz Festival: National and local jazz players. Coastal Jazz Association, 232-2222.

October:

Oktoberfest: Bavarian food festival on River Street.

Jewish Food Festival: Jewish food and music, Monterey Square.

Savannah Greek Festival: Greek food, music, and entertainment, Greek Orthodox Church.

November:

Christmas Made in the South: Big handicrafts market.

December:

"**Christmas in Savannah**" is a unique series of holidays events, including:

Christmas Tour of Homes: Tour of private homes decorated for Christmas.

Christmas at Colonial Wormsloe: A celebration of Christmas as it would have been in Savannah during the town's first year.

Tours

Guided and self-guided tours of the Historic District, the Victorian District, the low country areas, and a Negro Heritage Tour are available. Options include walking tours, driving tours, tape tours, carriage tours, and cruises, as well as special interest tours such as a Gallery Walk (233-7712), for art lovers, and tours for groups of children (p. 126). For information call the Savannah Visitors Center, 944-0456, or consult Sightseeing Tours in the yellow pages.

Resource Centers

For enrichment and research

Chatham County Public Library: 2002 Bull St., main branch. Telephone 234-5127. Book reviews, lectures, story hours.

Georgia Historical Society: 501 Whitaker St. Telephone 651-2128. Permanent, official library collection of Georgia history and architecture (p. 62).

Massie Heritage Interpretation Center: 207 East Gordon St. Telephone 651-7380. Studies in the city's built environment, architectural exhibitions, and special programs for students (p. 66).

Oatland Island Education Center: 711 Sandtown Rd. Telephone 897-3773. 175 acres environmental project (p. 125).

Marine Extension Service: Skidaway Island. Telephone 598-2496. Aquarium and exhibitions (p. 102).

Savannah Civic Center

Orleans Square at Montgomery St. and West Oglethorpe Avenue. Box Office 651-6556. Two auditoriums, one named after the famous Savannah musician Johnny Mercer and one after Martin Luther King, Jr. Miscellaneous events: Savannah Symphony concerts, ballet performances, gospel singing, rock bands, athletic events, circuses, conventions, and others.

Shopping Facilities

Savannah has scores of notable antique stores. A brochure including a map is available at the Visitors Center. Browse and enjoy.

Numerous interesting shops and galleries are gathered along Bull Street, in the heart of historic Savannah. Stroll down this most beautiful street for a pleasant shopping experience.

A variety of shops and galleries are located on River Street and in City Market.

The two malls are on the south side of town: Oglethorpe Mall, 7804 Abercorn St. Extension, and Savannah Mall, 14045 Abercorn St. Extension.

Broughton Street and its environs, once the major shopping center, are now the object of intense local revitalization efforts.

A Child's Guide to Savannah

Traveling with children can be a great pleasure—just imagine watching them how they explore a new place—if there are events and activities tailored specifically for children at the destination of your journey.

Savannah is the perfect city for a family vacation or for spouses and children to accompany the other member of the family on a business trip. Many of the attractions are city sponsored and free, while others may ask for small admission fees.

These are a few of the exciting possibilities for fun days in Savannah (with cross references to other pages). Have fun combining some of these wonderful possibilities, for instance a learning experience in a museum with playing outdoors at one of the many public playgrounds, or a visit to the forts with a trip to the beach.

Many museums, state parks and science centers have special children's programs. Check for times before you plan on them.

Science Museum: 4405 Paulsen St., Telephone 355-6705.
In the Exhibit Hall children find displays of minerals, animals and skeletons. In a 50 foot tower the museum houses a Foucault Pendulum. The Planetarium's presentations inform about the universe (special hours). The Museum's special Discovery Room, where

—Delia Solomons

children learn by playing, touching and exploring, is geared for ages 5 to 12. Puppet program. There are additional lectures, exhibits, field study trips and other programs for both adults and families throughout the year. Special summer program.

Telfair Mansion and Art Museum (p. 48): 121 Barnard St., Telephone: 232-1177.
The museum organizes quarterly on one Sunday afternoon a special program for the whole family with hands-on activities for children. Children's tours of different sections of the museum are available by reservation. In the summer the Telfair offers an arts program in different city parks followed by field trips to the museum for a fun interactive gallery and studio program. The museum also offers an interesting educative program for groups of children.

Central of Georgia Railway Roundhouse Complex (p. 27): 601 West Harris Street. With its display of model railroad sets and locomotives, it fulfills children's dreams.

Of special interest for many children is a visit to the **Birthplace of Juliette Gordon Low,** founder of the Girl Scouts (p. 50).

Other museums of interest for children are the **Train Museum** (p. 32) and the **Ships of the Sea Museum** (p. 32).

Aquarium: Skidaway Island (p. 102). Telephone 598-FISH.
The University of Georgia Marine Extension Service's facilities include an aquarium exhibiting over 200 live animals. Can be combined with a visit to the Skidaway Island State Park (p. 102).

—Delia Solomons

Libraries (p. 121): Libraries have story hours for children.

Forts: Children love to explore forts, and the Savannah area has four. Some of the forts also have a special children's program.

Fort Jackson (p. 91): Costumed reenactments and special programs, including special tours for children. For more information call 232-3945.

Fort Pulaski (p. 92): Special tours for children are available by reservation two weeks in advance. A staff member talks about the history of the fort on a child's level. For information and reservations call 786-5787.

Fort Screven (p. 92): On the North End of Tybee Island, the remains of this modern fort form part of the Tybee History Museum.

The visit of the three above mentioned forts can be combined with a trip to the beach of Tybee Island (p. 105) and/or the Oatland Island Education Center (see below).

Fort McAllister, State Historic Park (p. 92): Special tours for children are available but not all the time. For information call (912) 727-2339.

Nature experience with children:

Savannah National Wildlife Refuge (p. 108): For fans of alligators and indigenous nature of this area.

Oatland Island Education Center: 711 Sandtown Road, Telephone 897-3773.
Just off Islands Expressway, Highway 80. 175 acres. 1.5 miles of walking trails, animals indigenous to coastal Georgia in natural habitat setting, sheep, goats, cows, deer, birds, barn yard area; benches for bag lunch; special program for the public. Take insect repellent! Hours: Mon.-Fri. 8:30 a.m.-5 p.m., from Oct.-May, second Sat. in the month 11 a.m.-5 p.m.

You can combine your visit with a trip to the beach at Tybee Island (see below).

Tybee Island, Savannah's beach: A day at the beach is an exciting adventure for every child. Tybee Island offers a variety of landside activities if ocean and beach are not enough.

Tybee Island Marine Science Center: 1510 Strand, Tybee Island.
Besides the beach walks (p. 107) to which the whole family is invited, the Center offers a summertime children's program featuring sea camps. Children learn about the formation and development of the beach, erosions and the water life; arts and crafts are emphasized. The camps are held at special dates, run one week, and involve participation every afternoon. At other times, special children's afternoons are offered one day a week. Programs are subject to change. For information call 786-5917.

Tybee Lighthouse (p. 107): Climb the stairs for a terrific view of the Island.

In the environs of 16th Street are a water park, mini golf, and a classic amusement park, with games and rides for children, and picnic tables.

Tours of the city:

A carriage tour is a fun way for a child to see the city.

Explore Savannah: is a special tour service for groups of children (min. 14 persons). There are full day and half day "Activity Tours" and "Evening Outings" available, which show Savannah's historic highlights of particular interest to young people combined with other fun activities. Telephone 354-4560.

Another way to discover Savannah is a cruise on one of the cruise boats on the Savannah River (p. 121).

Playgrounds in parks and recreation areas

Lake Mayer Recreation Park: Montgomery Crossroad & Sallie Mood Dr. Fishing lake, boating, ducks to feed, pedal boat rental, playground, jogging and bicycle trail, basketball, tennis, picnic area, tournaments, concerts, rest rooms, wheelchair fitness court.

Daffin Park: 1500 East Victory Drive. Baseball, soccer, basketball, tennis, playgrounds, swimming pool, jogging path around the lake, picnic area, lake pavilion, fishing available for children, Grayson Stadium. Handicap accessible.

Forsyth Park: Gaston and Whitaker St. Playgrounds, tennis courts, softball fields, Fragrant Garden for the Blind.

Baseball Games: Grayson Stadium. Daffin Park at Victory Drive and Bee Road. Savannah Cardinals, professional baseball team, Telephone 351-9150.

—Delia Solomons

River Street (p. 32): River Street, with its bustle of tourist and commercial activities, is an attraction for any child: 1st Saturday of the month, arts and crafts fair, ships and tugs, cotton exchange, City Hall, cannon, museums, shopping, and Pirate's House.

Many of the festivals and parades mentioned earlier (p. 119) have special attractions for children or are just in general exciting for them, like a Night in Old Savannah, Georgia Heritage Celebration, outdoor concerts of the Savannah Symphony, Fireworks of the 4th of July, etc.

Summertime brings special activities for children, some free, some with a small admission fee. Programs include swimming, arts in the park, dancing, exercising, special events at playgrounds, threater, films, etc. For information consult the Leisure Service Bureau of the City of Savannah, 651-6783, the Artsline 233-ARTS, the Visitors Center 944-0456, or the newspaper.

Sports and Family Fun

Savannah offers a wide variety of outdoor recreation opportunities for all ages. For detailed information about facilities for any of the following, consult the Department of Leisure Services, 651-6783, on weekdays; or visit or call the Savannah Visitors Center, 944-0456; open seven days a week. Brochures available. Activities grouped on this page have cross references to other pages where they are described more fully.

- Major Recreation Parks
- Camp and Picnic Grounds
- Water Sports and Boating
- Riding
- Tennis
- Fishing
- Swimming
- Hunting
- Skating
- Golf
- Jogging

Team Sports: Baseball, basketball, softball, football.

Playgrounds: In addition to play areas provided at campgrounds and picnic areas, the city and county offer regularly scheduled playground activities year-round, with heaviest programs in summer. Games, arts and crafts, and sports are conducted at schools, neighborhood parks and recreation centers. For city events, call 651-6783.

Professional Baseball: See p. 126.

Tybee Mountain Waterslides: See p. 107.

Oatland Island Education Center: See p. 125.

Nature Trail: On the way to Tybee Island, see p. 105.

Allen E. Paulson Softball Complex: 5 deluxe fields. Field house.

Behind the Scenes

POPULATION: City: 137,560; Savannah area: 242,615.

LOCATION AND AREA: 24 miles from Atlantic Ocean on Savannah River. City: 60 square miles; county: 455 square miles.

PHYSICAL CHARACTERISTICS: Coastal plain. Almost level plateau, elevations from 0 to 50 ft. above sea level.

MAJOR TOWNS: Savannah, Pooler, Bloomingdale, Garden City, Port Wentworth, Thunderbolt, Vernonburg and Tybee Island.

CITY GOVERNMENT: Mayor, 8 Aldermen, City Manager.

CLIMATE: Average annual temperature 66.4 degrees. Highest mean 81.3 degrees, July; lowest mean 51.4 degrees, December. Average rainfall 51 inches. Average humidity 75%.

PORT: Southeast's leading foreign trade port between Baltimore and New Orleans.

TRANSPORTATION: Savannah has an International Airport. CSX & Norfolk Southern Railroads, Amtrak, Greyhound - Trailways, local bus system. U.S. 17, 17A, 80. Ga 21, I-16, I-95, I-516.

TELEVISION STATIONS: 5   **RADIO STATIONS**: 15

CHURCHES: Over 240, representing all major denominations.

EDUCATIONAL FACILITIES: 5 colleges, 52 public schools, 30 parochial and private, 1 vocational.

TENNIS COURTS: 50   **ROOMS**: 6710
GOLF COURSES: 3 Public   **ANNUAL VISITORS**: 5 Million
CAMPGROUNDS: 4

MEDICAL FACILITIES: Medical center for entire Coastal Empire. 5 hospitals; 9 nursing homes.

NEWSPAPERS: Savannah Morning News and Savannah Evening Press, daily. Four weekly, Islands Gazette, The Herald, The Savannah Tribune, and the Savannah Pennysaver.

INDUSTRY: 165 manufacturers. Major products: food, paper, chemicals, rubber, petroleum, wood products and transportation equipment.

MILITARY: The U.S. Army has over 4000 soldiers at Hunter Army Airfield.

EXCITEMENT JUST AHEAD: Downtown commercial district renovation.

Old Savannah Recipes

Old Savannah recipes, still favorites today: okra soup, Savannah red rice, beaten biscuits, strawberry preserves, iced tea and cold watermelon.

SAVANNAH OKRA SOUP

1   ham bone (or several ham hocks)
1   can beef consomme, undiluted
1½   quarts water
2   cups chopped celery
2   cups chopped onion
1   tablespoon each gumbo filet powder and Worchestershire Sauce
1   teaspoon each salt, pepper, Tabasco Sauce
2   cans tomato sauce
3   cups okra (fresh) or 2 packages frozen cut okra
1   teaspoon sugar

Put ham bone in large pot with 1½ quarts water, consomme, onion, celery and all seasonings. Bring to a boil, reduce heat to medium and cook for 30 minutes. Add okra, tomato sauce and 1 teaspoon sugar. Cook for one hour or more on low until well blended (may need more salt and pepper). Serve over steamed rice. You may serve fresh boiled shrimp or crab meat for a topping.

SAVANNAH RED RICE

4   slices bacon
1   medium onion, chopped
2   ribs celery, chopped
1   small bell pepper, chopped
2   cups raw rice, rinsed well
1   (1 lb.) can tomatoes, drained and chopped (reserve juice)
1   (8 oz.) can tomato sauce
1   teaspoon sugar
1   teaspoon salt
     Black pepper to taste
     Tabasco to taste (should be spicy)

Fry bacon in a heavy pot until crisp; remove. Saute onions, celery, bell pepper in bacon grease until onions are translucent. Crumble bacon; return to pot. Add rice; stir to coat with grease. Add tomatoes. Measure reserved tomato juice and tomato sauce; add water to make 2½ cups (total) liquid. Pour over rice and bring to a boil, stirring occasionally. Immediately lower heat until barely simmering, cover pot and set timer for 20 minutes. After 20 minutes, remove from heat and let sit at least 20 minutes. Do not peek. After 20 minutes, fluff with a fork and serve.

(Recipe reprinted by the courtesy of **The Pirates' House Cookbook**)

The cradle of applied botany
is here in Savannah!

LIVE OAK

The South's Post Card Tree

Flora
and Fauna

On February 25, 1937, a resolution of the Georgia General Assembly made the Live Oak Georgia's official tree. This beautiful tree flourishes along the coastal plains and islands where the first settlers of the State resided.

And the hands that rocked the cradle nurtured America's first agricultural experimental garden, a ten-acre plot named Trustees' Garden in 1733 by James Edward Oglethorpe in honor of his fellow Englishmen who were the Trustees of the infant colony of Georgia.

Encouraged by the Apothecaries' Garden at Chelsea, England, Trustees' Garden flourished for ten years after the planting of living specimens of flowers, herbs, trees and vines from Europe, the Far East and the Caribbean Isles. In addition, many extraordinary native flora were discovered and carefully cultivated. From early experiments the South's "King Cotton" was born—sharing the lime-light with the Georgia peach, the South's most famous fruit.

Listed on the following pages are the most common varieties of trees and plants which may be seen growing in Savannah and her coastal environs. Many of these, as descendants of the earliest colonial flora, thrive as living tributes to the diligence and imagination of Savannah's 18th century horticulturists.

TREES

AMERICAN HOLLY (Ilex opaca). Familiar to all. Red berries in fall, shiny green leaves.

CRAPE MYRTLE (Lagerstroemia indica). Big shrub or small tree. Blooms all summer. Lush six petaled 1½ inch flower resembling crinkled white, pink or purple crepe paper.

DOGWOOD (Cornus florida). Boughs in flat irregular layers. White blossoms in spring.

LIVE OAK (Quercus virginiana). Small, smooth oval leaves. Massive limbs, usually draped with Spanish Moss. State tree of Georgia, lives 200-300 years.

LOBLOLLY PINE (Pinus taeda). Leading commercial timber species, 6-9 inch needles growing three together, fast growing to 60-90 feet.

LONGLEAF PINE (Pinus palustris). Needles longest in the world—up to 18 inches. Timber for heavy construction.

MAGNOLIA (Magnolia grandiflora). Large tree. Glossy leaves. Creamy, 8-12" fragrant blossoms in early summer.

MIMOSA (Albizia julibrissin). Spreading branches, ferny foliage and "powder-puff" pink blooms.

PALMETTO or CABBAGE PALM (Sabal palmetto). Branchless trunk to 90 ft. with headdress of huge fan-like leaves.

REDBUD or JUDAS TREE (Cercis canadensis). A small, sturdy, irregular tree. Afroth with pinkish-purple flowers in spring. Round, heart-shaped leaves.

SAVANNAH HOLLY (Ilex opaca savannah). A variety of American Holly discovered in Savannah and seen along coastal Georgia.

SLASH PINE (Pinus elliottii). Straight, branchless trunk crowned abruptly with angled limbs, 10 inch needles.

SWEET BAY MAGNOLIA (Magnolia virginiana). Leaves, oval. Small white flowers, exquisitely fragrant.

SWEET GUM (Liquidambar styraciflua). Star-shaped leaves, the size of maple leaves. Seed pods like thorny balls.

OTHER TREES

BALD CYPRESS (Taxodium distichum).
CAMPHOR TREE (Cinnamomum camphora).
CHERRY LAUREL (Prunus caroliniana).
GINKGO (Ginkgo biloba).
LOQUAT (Eriobotrya japonica).
PECAN (Carya illinoiensis).
PERSIMMON (Diospyros virginiana).

SHRUBS

AZALEAS (Azalea indica). Most common are "Formosa," "G.L. Taber" and "Fielder's White." Evergreen foliage. Flamboyant petals bloom from early spring to mid-April.

BAMBOO (Bambusa multiplex). "Clump-type." Often 15 feet in height. Graceful, slender stems.

CAMELLIAS (Many varieties). Colorful from early fall till late spring. Coastal garden favorites.

COMMON OLEANDER (Nerium oleander). May grow to twenty feet; always shrubby looking. Long, gray-green leaves. Summer flowers in single or double clusters of white, pink or rose, yellow or salmon.

PITTOSPORUM (Pittosporum tobira). Bright, evergreen with shiny foliage. Spring clusters of fragrant white or pale yellow flowers. Commonly used for hedges. (P.T. variegata). Cream and grey-green foliage.

PODOCARPUS or YEW (Podocarpus macrophyllus). Dark everygreen 2 to 3 inch narrow leaves; fine to medium texture.

PYRACANTHA or FIRETHORN (Pyracantha koidzumi). Extremely popular and versatile. Dense, twiggy, irregular thorny bush. Flat clusters of white spring flowers. Heavy bunches of bright orange fruits in fall and winter.

SPANISH BAYONET (Yucca aloifolia). Coarse-textured, sword-like, evergreen leaves. Bold white plumes of summer flowers.

OTHER COMMON SHRUBS

ALTHAEA (Hibiscus syriacus).

CAPE PLUMBAGO (Plumbago capensis).

FEIJOA or PINEAPPLE GUAVA (Feijoa sellowiana).

HYDRANGEA (Hydrangea macrophylla).

JAPANESE PRIVET (Ligustrum japonicum).

LITTLELEAF JAPANESE BOX (Boxus microphylla japonica).

SPIREA (S. prunifolia, S. thunbergi, S. cantoniensis, S. van houttei).

SWEET VIBURNUM (Viburnum odoratissimum).

THORNY ELAEAGNUS (Elaeagnus pungens).

Magnolia

VINES

ALGERIAN IVY (Hedera canariensis). Large, lush foliage, vigorous growth.

BANKSIA or LADY BANKS ROSE (Rosa banksiae). Fine textured evergreen foliage, practically thornless. Creamy yellow flowers.

CAROLINA JESSAMINE (Gelsemium sempervirens). Small and fine textured foliage. Bright golden masses of trumpet-like early spring flowers.

CHEROKEE ROSE (Rosa laevigata). State flower of Georgia. Rich, glossy, semi-evergreen foliage and single 3-4" white flowers. Long blooming season in spring and short in fall.

CHINESE WISTERIA (Wisteria sinensis). Coarse in foliage texture and habit of growth. Large flowers, white, pink or purple.

CLIMBING FIG (Ficus pumila). Clothes any wall with a close fitting mat of greenery.

OTHER VINES

Holly

CONFEDERATE or STAR JASMINE (Trachelospermum jasminoides).
CORAL VINE (Antigonon leptopus).
ENGLISH IVY (Hedera helix).
PASSION FLOWER (Passiflora incarnata).
SOUTHERN SMILAX (Smilax lanceolata).
SWEETAUTUMN CLEMATIS (Clematis paniculata).

SPANISH MOSS (Tillandsia usneoides). A graceful herb, a "changeling" of the pineapple family. Not a true moss but an air plant, using trees and telegraph wires for support. Has many long, slender moss-like stems which bear small leaves and pale green flowers.

GROUNDCOVER PLANTS

BIG BLUE LIRIOPE (Liriope muscari). Grows in clumps. Dark, narrow evergreen leaves about 12 inches long. Summer spikes of violet flowers.

DWARF LILYTURF (Mondo japonicus). About 4 inches tall. Forms broad expanses of fine textured leaves.

CARPET BUGLE (Ajuga reptans). Evergreen foliage with a purplish tinge, about 3 inches high, blooms blue spikes in summer.

PERIWINKLE (Vinca minor)

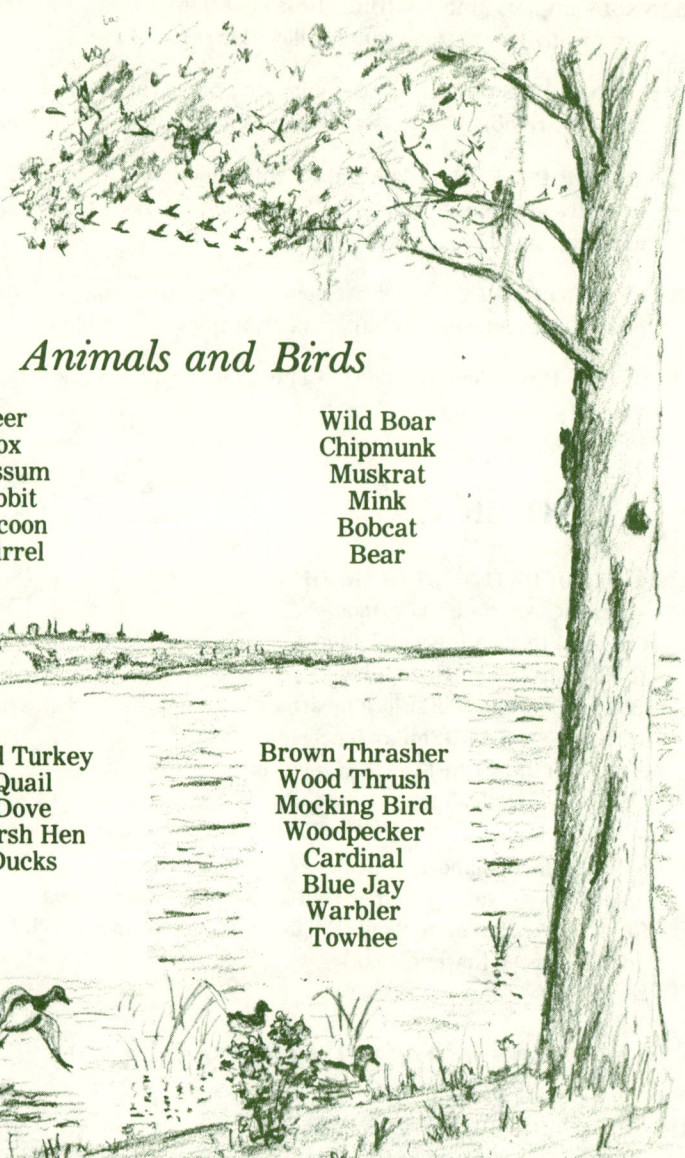

Animals and Birds

Deer
Fox
Opossum
Rabbit
Raccoon
Squirrel

Wild Boar
Chipmunk
Muskrat
Mink
Bobcat
Bear

Wild Turkey
Quail
Dove
Marsh Hen
Ducks

Brown Thrasher
Wood Thrush
Mocking Bird
Woodpecker
Cardinal
Blue Jay
Warbler
Towhee

—Drawing by Gerald Storey

Index

(137)

The work of two of Savannah's most revered artists, now deceased, appears frequently throughout the pages of this book.

LEONORA QUARTERMAN: 1911-1979. Established as one of the outstanding watercolor artists in the South, Miss Quarterman produced uniquely detailed silk screen prints of her native Savannah and of coastal scenes. She held one man shows in Savannah and Winston Salem and at Emory University, and exhibited her work throughout the South and at the Smithsonian Institute. See index for page numbers of her paintings.

CHRISTOPHER MURPHY: 1902-1973. As a native Savannahian, Mr. Murphy created remarkably sensitive drawings which capture the beauty of his city and the coastal landscape. The originals for his book SAVANNAH, produced with a text by Walter C. Hartridge, were exhibited in a one man show at the Telfair Academy in 1947; a retrospective exhibition of his work in 1974 drew the largest attendance ever recorded at the Telfair. See index for page numbers of his drawings. For originals and reproductions, call Christopher Murphy Studio, 232-4796.

—Painting by Leonora Quarterman

SAVANNAH'S "GINGERBREAD" HOUSE
On Bull Street at 36th Street